The Martini Companion

The Martini Companion
A Connoisseur's Guide

Gary Regan and Mardee Haidin Regan

Photographs by Steve Belkowitz

RUNNING PRESS
PHILADELPHIA · LONDON

Dedication

This book is dedicated to our mothers,

Vi Regan and Gladys Hilgert, and our aunts,

Mary Armstrong, Evelyn Hackney, and Anne Haidin

—each one a cocktail in her own right.

———— ((()) ————

© 1997 by Gary Regan and Mardee Haidin Regan
Photographs © 1997 by Steve Belkowitz

Printed in China

9   8   7   6   5   4   3   2

Digit on the right indicates the number
of this printing

Library of Congress Cataloging-in-Publication Number 96-71609
ISBN 0-7624-0061-7

This book may be ordered by mail from the publisher.
Please include $2.50 for postage and handling.
But try your bookstore first!

Running Press Book Publishers
125 South Twenty-second Street
Philadelphia, Pennsylvania 19103-4399

Contents

Acknowledgments

Many people were key in producing this book: First and foremost, major thanks go to our friends "Rowdy" Ray Foley, publisher of *Bartender* magazine, and "Saintly" Stephen Visakay, collector extraordinaire of vintage barware and cocktail shakers. Without Ray's generosity in letting us pore through his library we never would have been able to prove the origin of the Dry Martini—that proof came as much from Ray as it did from us. Without Steve Visakay's equally generous access to his astounding collection, the photographs for this book would not include most of the gorgeous antique pieces within.

Within the spirits industry, Hugh Williams, master distiller of gins for United Distillers in England, went to a tremendous amount of trouble to explain how gin is made, and he also loaned us his copies of some of the rarer texts on the subject.

We could fill half this book by telling you of others who helped with specific products, but we hope that the following people will forgive us for merely mentioning their names here. If there are any inaccuracies in this book, let the blame fall on our heads, and if we failed to mention anyone who helped, please accept our apologies: Peter Angus, Lisa Appleby, Harry Arpadi, Laura

Baddish, Trisha Barroll, Carol Basso-Pagano, Charles Kemmis Betty, Florence Boissière, Peter Bordeaux, Joanne Burston, Dan Buttling, Tom Coppini, Jennifer Crowl, Sarah Dale, Samara Farber, Mark Fish, Deborah French, Alice Gallagher, Mark Gothberg, Bevin Gove, Becky Green, Sean Harrison, Don Hazlewood, Chris Hoffman, Fred Horowitz, Barbara Waits Juckett, Jeff Kanbar, Steve Kaufman, Kathy Law, Arlene Lederman, Teresa Maloney, Chris Massey, Marie Massey, Fred Miranda, Chris Morris, Carl Nolet, Susan Overton, Paul Pacult, Gino Palazzolo, Jeff Pogash, Brian Robinson, Gil Rosenberg, Michel Roux, Karin Timpone, Bob Shack, Martin Slattery, Alan Snelling, Keith Steer, Margaret Stern, Meg Syberg, Mike Veach, John Vidal, Stephan Wilkinson, and Sue Woodley.

As always, thanks to Michael Carlisle, our guardian angel at the William Morris Agency, Inc., in New York. The people at Running Press—from Martini lovers Buz and Janet Bukovinsky Teacher to Nancy Steele—have had no end of patience. The Design department, designers Maria Taffera Lewis and Frances J. Soo Ping Chow, were ever enthusiastic as were photographer Steve Belkowitz and his team, Beth and Sam Belkowitz and the indispensable Dawn Bradley. Finally, special, profuse thanks to our very own, wise, spirited, and all-around wonderful editor, Tara Ann McFadden.

Introduction

———◆◇◆———

For some it's the crocus or daffodil, for others the initial sighting of a robin redbreast; for us, though, it's less substantive, but oh, the joy of the first Martini of spring! Not that we deny ourselves Martinis through the winter, but sometime between taxes and mid-May, one day we wake to the sun streaming through the windows; the birds are chirping a little louder; and after the first cup of coffee, we rush to the freezer to make sure our Martini glasses are chilling. Tonight's the night. We manage—just—to work through the day. Then, at around two, one of us will make a trip to the pantry—do we have olives? The first Martini of spring deserves a fresh jar of olives. With luck and determination we will last until around 4:37.

"Well, dear, we started a little early this morning—want to close down for the day?"

"Oh, um, well, yes, please." Ten minutes later we can be found sitting on the deck and then, at last, we sip our Martinis. And oh, how we smile.

The Art of the Martini

---·--·---

I T IS IMPOSSIBLE TO MAKE A DRY MARTINI
without the correct accoutrements. Martinis cannot
be assembled in mason jars, they can't be stirred with a
chopstick, and they simply mustn't be strained through
the sieve that is normally used for rice. This is not true
of all cocktails; allegedly, the Screwdriver was born using
the actual tool, but the Martini is a demanding sophisti-
cate, and only the best will do. It must be treated with
respect from the very moment that you conceive the
notion that a Martini is called for, and if you dare even
to think of, say, a Long Island Iced Tea while you are
preparing a Martini, you should retire immediately and
rest until you have regained your taste and senses.

You might love shaken Martinis or insist on lovingly
stirring the ingredients. No matter. We are not here to
judge. We will endeavor to explain how to make the
drink using either method, but by the end of this chapter
you will know exactly how to make a proper Martini.

GLASSWARE

Martinis should be served in cocktail glasses—that is, the elegant V-shaped glass atop a slim stem that is often referred to as a Martini glass. If you serve a Martini over ice in an Old-Fashioned or rocks glass, it becomes a totally new drink, known in the best circles as an abomination. Select a cocktail glass with the thinnest of rims, and if you are entertaining deserving guests, be sure to have two sizes of glass on hand. The larger glass will be used to serve the first Martini of the evening, and depending on the mood of the assembly, you can select smaller glasses at any given point for subsequent cocktails. You are not being judgmental or mean by switching to smaller glasses; the point is that a Martini should be very, very cold when consumed, and although a large Martini served as the first drink of the evening will probably make its way down parched throats rather rapidly, subsequent cocktails, if called for at all, are usually consumed at a much slower pace.

Martini glasses should always be well chilled before service. The preferred and easiest method is to chill them in the freezer for a minimum of four hours. When necessary, however, they can be chilled with ice and water as follows: Place the glasses in the sink and fill each with ice cubes; turn on the cold tap and allow the water to run in a continuous stream into the glass so that it overflows and spills out over the sides. Turn the water off and leave the glasses there while you concoct the drink. At the last possible moment, vigorously shake the chilled glass so that the iced water, once again, spills over the outside. Pick up each glass by the stem and pour out the ice and water. Before you fill the glass, however, you must take hold of the stem and shake out any water that clings to the interior. This method is acceptable only when the freezer is bereft of chilled glasses.

THE SHAKEN MARTINI

One of us thinks that shaking Martinis is completely unacceptable, a silly method of mixing the drink that results in a watery, if very cold, poor substitute for an otherwise perfect drink. The other thinks that the coldest Martini is the primary goal, and thus any method that leads to that end is just fine indeed. (If it were possible to inject Freon, liquid nitrogen, or whatever substance is the coldest thing in the world, and doing so didn't hurt you—or the drink—then, marvelous, we want some.)

The stirrer-preferrer claims that when a drink is shaken, the ice cubes clatter together with such turbulence that small shards of ice chip off the cubes, melt, and dilute the Martini cocktail far more than is "permissible." God forbid that an unmelted shard of ice or two should make its way into the glass and dilute the drink even more. The other pooh-poohs that claim by using scientific methods: Three shards were arranged on a mirror and left to melt. When all three were combined, they amounted to but a single droplet of water. The more persnickety of us would have cheered riotously if double agent Vesper Lynd had bludgeoned James Bond to death for having the audacity to order his Martini shaken. While one of us holds that Vesper Martinis (see page 170) should be shaken and then tossed away, the other suggests trying one (the combination of gin and vodka with Lillet is delightful)—just be sure it's very cold.

If you must shake your Martinis, you will need a cocktail shaker, complete with a lid or spout that is fitted with a strainer. Do not, under any circumstances, use a Boston Shaker—the two cones, one metal, the other glass—that most professional bartenders use. You may accept a Martini shaken in a Boston shaker at a bar, and this piece of equipment is very acceptable for making any other drink at home—but not a Martini. When selecting a cocktail shaker, we suggest that you choose an antique, preferably one in Art Deco style. You need an instrument with a memory. You need a device that has shaken Martinis in days gone by, one that can recall the shouts of "Here's how!" at a pre-Prohibition bar. You need an accomplice.

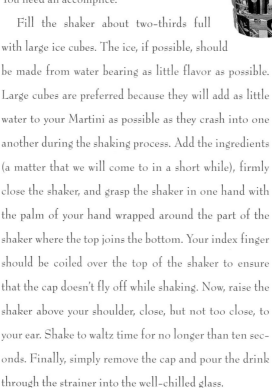

Fill the shaker about two-thirds full with large ice cubes. The ice, if possible, should be made from water bearing as little flavor as possible. Large cubes are preferred because they will add as little water to your Martini as possible as they crash into one another during the shaking process. Add the ingredients (a matter that we will come to in a short while), firmly close the shaker, and grasp the shaker in one hand with the palm of your hand wrapped around the part of the shaker where the top joins the bottom. Your index finger should be coiled over the top of the shaker to ensure that the cap doesn't fly off while shaking. Now, raise the shaker above your shoulder, close, but not too close, to your ear. Shake to waltz time for no longer than ten seconds. Finally, simply remove the cap and pour the drink through the strainer into the well-chilled glass.

THE STIRRED MARTINI

We agree that in order to make a first-rate Martini, you must do so lovingly; you must show a little respect for the drink. Stirring a Martini is a contemplative exercise that requires great concentration. One of us complains that when shaking a Martini, the ice cubes create so much noise at the side of your head that concentration is impossible; the other sides with the aforementioned waltz theory: The clatter is replaced by the music in your head. Naturally, the waltz thesis can be applied while stirring as well.

As you stir, visions of an elegant past—one that you might never actually have lived through—should enter your mind. You will hear the soft sounds of the ice cubes as they glide by each other, sometimes kissing, often just flirting, and the energy created by the fusion of the ingredients in the pitcher will travel to your fingers, slowly make its way up your arm, and enter your very soul.

Seek an antique Martini pitcher complete with a long glass rod for stirring. Choose only the tallest pitcher you can find, preferably one made from the finest crystal, and make sure that the lip of the pitcher, designed to catch the ice as you pour your cocktails, is of sufficient substance to prevent large ice cubes from

falling into the glass. Fill the pitcher with large ice cubes to around the two-thirds mark, add the ingredients, and stir gently—clockwise—for at least twenty and no more than thirty seconds. (If you are counting the revolutions, stir for an odd number of turns.) That's the technique for making a stirred Martini.

INGREDIENTS

Gin or vodka? Vermouth or no? Bitters of any kind? A dash of Pernod, perhaps? These are the Martini questions. The gin, vodka, and vermouth questions are, of course, common to all Martini makers, but the bitters, Pernod, or any other ingredient are not normally considered. With a respectful nod to the past, however, we sometimes make Martinis with a dash or two of orange bitters, and Angostura bitters make an interesting variation, provided they are added in minuscule amounts: Sprinkle just one dash over the ice, swirl it around for a couple of seconds, and then strain it off before adding the other ingredients.

Pernod, or any other absinthe substitute, such as Ricard or Herbsaint, is another story. Often true absinthe, made illegal in most countries prior to World War I, was added to Dry Martinis in turn-of-the-century London gentlemen's clubs, but that product was far drier than the substitutes we use today. A Dry Martini with a splash of that delectable liquor was incredibly pungent and we understand why those English gents opted for a dash or two in their drinks. By using a substitute, however, and using it very sparingly—one dash at most—we are reminded of that wonderful bygone era, and we highly recommend that you at least give this drink a try.

THE BASICS: VERMOUTH AND GIN OR VODKA

Vermouth, once opened, should be stored in the refrigerator. We highly recommend that you buy small bottles—375 ml—unless you use a lot of vermouth in your Martinis or your household consumes at least eight Martinis on a daily basis. As a general rule, vermouth kept at cool temperatures will not oxidize noticeably for at least three months, and some companies claim that their vermouths will stay fresh for half a year. We have never kept a bottle of vermouth for that length of time and therefore can't comment.

The quantity of vermouth that should be added to a Martini is a question best left to the individual. Though we have our own opinion (see below), we think the vermouth controversy is part of the beauty of the Martini. Martinis give us the opportunity to show the world what freedom of choice is all about. In *An Alphabet for Gourmets*, author M. F. K. Fisher suggests (in more eloquent words than these) that the Martini is to America what vodka is to Russia, and we could not agree more. So what point is there for us to tell you how much vermouth to put into your Martini? You will make it with as much or as little as you please.

Vermouth antics abound: Some people pour the vermouth into the pitcher, swirl it around for a while, and then discard the liquid; others spritz their Martini glasses with vermouth kept in an atomizer. (Tiffany makes a lovely one in sterling silver.) Some folks soak their olives or onions in vermouth. We have found, though, that gin Martinis made with approximately eight parts gin to one part vermouth, and vodka Martinis made from six parts vodka to one part vermouth, are best—try it and see.

Another variable that matters in Martini-making is the brand of gin or vodka and vermouth you use. Some gins are more pungent than others, and even though vodkas are meant to be flavorless, they do differ from brand to brand. Vermouths vary widely—you'll need to taste several. Whatever gin or vodka you choose, store it at room temperature, not in the refrigerator or freezer. There is good reason for this: We have already argued that Martinis on the rocks are not acceptable because they can become too diluted; however, Martinis *should and must* be diluted to a certain extent. If you use cold gin or vodka, not enough ice will melt into the drink for it to be a real, properly made Martini. The amount of chilled vermouth added to the drink is a small but necessary evil. Now this may shock you, but it's a fact: If you pour a total of three ounces of gin or vodka and vermouth into an ice-filled pitcher and stir the mixture for the prescribed twenty to thirty seconds, the Martini that you strain into your glass will measure—give or take a little and depending on whether you are mixing the drink in Nome, Alaska, or Key West, Florida—an astonishing four ounces in capacity. That's right, a true Dry Martini is one-fourth water, and this is the only way to drink a Martini.

Literary Martini drinkers

RUSSELL BAKER

ROBERT BENCHLEY

AUNTIE MAME DENNIS

M. F. K. FISHER

F. SCOTT FITZGERALD

IAN FLEMING

DASHIELL HAMMETT

ERNEST HEMINGWAY

JACK LONDON

W. SOMERSET MAUGHAM

H. L. MENCKEN

OGDEN NASH

DOROTHY PARKER

EVELYN WAUGH

E. B. WHITE

TENNESSEE WILLIAMS

HERMAN WOUK

GARNISHES

It used to be that when ordering a Martini, you would specify your preference for a lemon twist or an olive; in the case of a Gibson, one or more pearl onions would automatically be added to your drink. Those days are long gone. Now you may select from a wide range of garnishes, including a caper berry, a sprig of tarragon, a basil leaf, a pickled walnut, an olive stuffed with an almond, an anchovy, a chile pepper, or whatever else some entrepreneur has decided to stuff into our little green friend. We have our preferences and you have yours, but still, there are rules with garnishes that must be followed.

Olives must be green—ripe (black) olives are abhorrent to the serious Martini drinker. Olives must be pitted—to avoid chipped teeth. Generally, small green olives are preferred, but if you're feeling frisky and can find very large green olives, you can do what our friend R. F. Starling does and host a Marbiggi party. As to the number of olives that should be served in a Martini, keep in mind that this is a cocktail, not a salad; you don't want the olives to displace too much of the luscious liquid. Again, it's best to stick with an odd number—either one or three.

Lemon twists should be pared from well-washed and dried fresh lemons. To make a proper lemon twist, first cut a slice from one end of the lemon and stand the fruit on what has now become its base. Take a sharp paring knife and cut off a thin strip of peel, incorporating just a bit of the white inner pith but not enough to reveal the interior fruit. The twist should be at least one-half inch wide and as long as the lemon allows. Tallish lemons are preferred. Take the lemon twist and hold it, yellow side down, about three inches above the surface of the drink; gently twist the lemon peel to release its precious oil, which will float down and rest atop the drink. Now gently rub the yellow side of the twist all around the rim of the glass, and then drop the twist into the drink.

We have not yet formulated specific rules to govern pickled walnuts, tarragon, or chile peppers, we only suggest that these garnishes be either as fresh as possible or stored in a manner suggested by the manufacturer.

Any garnish that you choose should be added *after* the Martini has been poured, and there is good reason for this: It may be that you have mixed a slightly larger cocktail than you had intended, and should the liquid reach all the way up to the rim of the glass, its eyes just peeping over the top, you will have no room for the garnish. It is far better to serve the garnish on the side than to leave any of your precious Martini to waste away in the pitcher or slop over the side of the glass.

PERFECT DRY MARTINIS

We have already explained that we do, on occasion, make ourselves variations on the Martini, but the instructions that follow govern what we consider to be perfect Dry Martinis in the "new" traditional style. The "old" traditional style called for equal parts of vermouth and gin.

We also have discussed our favorite ratios of spirits to vermouth (8:1 for gin, 6:1 for vodka), and you know that our Martinis are consumed without ice, so what is there left to say? Only this: One of us prefers gin Martinis with one unstuffed olive, and the other is more likely to drink vodka Martinis with a twist of lemon. Neither of us balks at a Gibson—gin or vodka—and we both think that caper berries make excellent garnishes. And while we are confessing our sins: Although we believe that a Martini should never be served over ice, coldness is its most important quality. Thus, when we have been silly enough to be talking instead of drinking and our cocktails have become just a little too warm, we will not hesitate to add a solitary ice cube to a half-finished drink. Then, we stir it briefly and slug it right back—it's far better than sipping a warm Martini.

The History of Martinis

---◄○/○/○►---

AS IS THE CASE WITH MANY OF THE WORLD'S cocktails, the origins of the Martini and the Dry Martini are indefinite. Theories abound as to who was the first person to perform the ceremony wherein gin first said, "I do," to its never-blushing bride, dry vermouth. One tale holds that the Martini cocktail got its name from Martini and Rossi vermouth, and indeed, many bartending guides of the 1920s and 1930s called specifically for that brand; however, most of the earlier Martini recipes don't mention any brand names whatsoever. Another tale claims that the cocktail was named after the Martini and Henry rifle, because the drink, like the gun, had such a hefty "kick." Again, though, the story doesn't quite ring true.

In *Stirred-Not Shaken: The Dry Martini*, author John Doxat told the story of Martini di Arma di Taggia, head bartender at New York City's Knickerbocker Hotel, making the world's first Dry Martini for oil magnate John D. Rockefeller in 1910. The story, which at first glance is extremely plausible, came from oil executive James Porter, who in the early 1970s recorded a conversation with "Luigi," a man who had tended bar with di Taggia. Luigi claimed that his story was true, and surely he believed every word of it, but the Dry Martini was mentioned by name before 1910, so it couldn't have been the first.

The whole town of Martinez, California, also lays claim to knowing the true origin of the Martini, and according to the Martinez Area Chamber of Commerce, the drink dates to 1849, when a gold miner, en route to San Francisco and on top of the world after striking gold, ordered champagne in a popular Martinez bar. Having no champagne on hand, the bartender offered to make the man a Martinez Special—three parts gin and one part "dry sauterne," garnished with an olive.

A variation on this story was told in the 1950s by the town's former fire chief, John M. "Toddy" Briones. Briones claimed that it was his brother-in-law, Julio Richelieu, who created the Martini in 1874. His version of the tale had it that a miner visited Richelieu's bar and requested a bottle of whiskey. Richelieu, according to Briones, persuaded the miner to try something different and made the world's first Dry Martini for him. A 1992 article by Steven LaVoie in the *Oakland Tribune*, however, states that the Martinez Chamber of Commerce concocted this story in 1953 and used Briones to verify the tale. (We should add here that the Martinez Chamber of Commerce is staffed with wonderfully friendly people, who when asked about the Martini story, plant their tongues firmly in their cheeks.)

In 1983, a mock court hearing was held at the Martinez City Council chambers in an attempt to overturn a San Francisco mock court decision that the Martini had been created in Fog City. Jerry Thomas, a famous bartender of the 1860s who plied his trade at San Francisco's Occidental Hotel, had been cited by the San Franciscans as having created the Martinez in or around 1862 for a customer who stopped by the bar on his way to the town of Martinez. However, in *Straight Up or On the Rocks,* author William Grimes states that the Martinez cocktail did not appear in print until 1884, and it wasn't included in any version of Thomas's book, originally titled *How to Mix Drinks or The Bon Vivant's Companion,* until the 1887 edition. Although there is no mention of the Martinez in the first printing of Thomas's book (1862), in a 1928 edition, editor Herbert Asbury stated in the introduction that the Martini was originally known as the Martinez.

Unfortunately, the true origin of the Martini—sweet or dry—doesn't include any flamboyant bartenders that we can name; in fact, if we were to credit any individual at all, that person would have to be Charles Darwin, for certainly the Dry Martini is the result of evolution. The way we see it: The Manhattan spawned the Martinez, which sired the Martini, which evolved into the Dry Martini.

An 1884 bar book by O. H. Byron includes reference to the Martinez, describing it as a Manhattan in which gin is substituted for whiskey. Many other recipes for the Martinez, from the late nineteenth and early twentieth centuries describe the Martinez in either exactly the same way as did Byron, or if you compare their recipes for the Manhattan and the Martinez, you find them to be identical, with one exception: The Martinez used gin as its base liquor and the Manhattan used whiskey. Thus, wasn't the Martinez merely a *variation* on the Manhattan, just as the Brandy Alexander is a variation on the original gin-based Alexander cocktail?

Recipes from *The Bar-Tender's Guide* by Jerry Thomas
(The order of the ingredients has been altered.)

Manhattan Cocktail	Martinez Cocktail
3 dashes Boker's bitters	1 dash Boker's bitters
2 dashes Curaçao or Maraschino	2 dashes Maraschino
1 pony of rye whiskey	1 pony of Old Tom gin
1 wine-glass of vermouth	1 wine-glass of vermouth
2 small lumps of ice	2 small lumps of ice

The instructions for making these drinks differ only inasmuch as the Manhattan is shaken and strained into a claret glass, whereas the Martinez is shaken and strained into a cocktail glass.

Curaçao, maraschino liqueur, orange bitters, Angostura bitters, Boker's bitters (now unavailable), and gomme, or gum syrup (sugar water) were all very popular in the late 1800s. A small amount of one or the other was added to almost every cocktail recipe.

The evolution of the Martini spins on two points— The style of the gin and the type of vermouth used to make it: Three different styles of gin were available— Genever, or Hollands gin, a heavy-bodied somewhat sweetish spirit; Old Tom, a sweetened London gin; and London dry gin, the type we use to make our Dry Martinis today. Very many recipes from that period call specifically for Old Tom gin. As for the vermouth, in those days it was common parlance to refer to sweet vermouth as "Italian," and to dry vermouth as "French." Most recipes from the late 1800s call for "vermouth," without specifying dry or sweet.

Indeed, all the recipes for the Manhattan printed prior to 1895 merely called for "vermouth," but in that year a recipe appears for the "Manhattan Cocktail, Extra Dry," in *Modern American Drinks*, by George Kappeler. He instructs, "Mix the same as the Manhattan Cocktail . . . and use dry vermouth in place of sweet." Similarly, in 1903, V. B. Lewis gave two Manhattan recipes in his book, *The Complete Buffet Guide or How To Mix All Kinds of Drinks*; one was made with sweet vermouth, the other with dry. We've concluded that, prior to 1895, when a recipe called for "vermouth," the author was referring to the sweet style.

The first recipe for a Martini appears in *New and Improved Illustrated Bartender's Manual or How To Mix Drinks of the Present Style* (1888) by Harry Johnson of New York City. But this recipe is basically the same as earlier recipes for the Martinez cocktail—Old Tom gin and sweet vermouth, as well as gum syrup, bitters, and curaçao. Similarly, Kappeler's 1895 book includes a Martini recipe, and it too, is made from the same ingredients that other bartenders were using to make a Martinez—proof positive that the names "Martini" and "Martinez" were, to some extent, interchangeable during the last years of the 1800s. The first drinks to be called Martinis were actually Martinez cocktails—the name was changing, but the ingredients were the same.

In 1903, however, we see two recipes for the Martinez in Lewis's book. Actually, Lewis gives two Manhattan recipes—one using sweet vermouth, the

other dry—and under "Martinez," he simply states, "Same as either of the two Manhattans, only you substitute gin for whiskey." His "dry vermouth" version of the Manhattan, however, also included bitters and gum syrup, so although we now have a Martinez made with dry vermouth, it was still a sweetened drink, and he failed to specify whether he wanted us to make it with London dry or Old Tom gin.

The first recipe for a Dry Martini cocktail that meets our definition was printed in *Louis Mixed Drinks With Hints for the Care & Serving of Wines* (1906) by Louis Muckenstrum. In this book, Muckenstrum details a "Martini Cocktail," which, for all intents and purposes is a Martinez—sweet vermouth, maraschino liqueur, Old Tom gin, etc.—and a "Dry Martini Cocktail" made from dry vermouth, dry gin, a couple of dashes of orange bitters, and a dash of curaçao. "Wait a minute," you say, "a Dry Martini with bitters and curaçao?" But the fact is, most Dry Martinis contained orange bitters right up until the 1940s. Muckenstrum's book, in our opinion, marks a turning point, and just as our forefathers would balk at the idea of a Dry Martini made with less than one-third dry vermouth, they would also insist on at least a dash of orange bitters.

In or around 1906, the modern Dry Martini was born. It evolved from the original sweet Martini (or Martinez), and that drink was, as we have seen, a variation on the Manhattan. Louis Muckenstrum was the first to print the recipe.

Right up to the beginning of Prohibition, bar manuals repeated a variety of directives for the Manhattan, the Martinez, and the Martini. In 1913, *Angostura Bitters Complete Mixing Guide* detailed a recipe for a Manhattan Cocktail comprised of whiskey, vermouth, and orange bitters, Angostura bitters, and simple syrup; directly below that recipe were directions for making a Martinez Cocktail: "Prepare the same as a Manhattan Cocktail, substituting gin for whiskey." The following year saw the publication of *Drinks* by Jacques Straub, "formerly wine steward of the Blackstone, Chicago, and the Pendennis Club, Louisville," and his book included a Dry Martini made solely from equal parts of dry vermouth and dry gin. It also gave the exact same ingredients for a drink that he called a "Gibson Cocktail." There were no pearl onions in Straub's Gibson, an addition that was probably made in the 1930s at New York's Players Club, but nevertheless, a cocktail called the Gibson, made from dry gin and dry vermouth, did exist in 1914, and Straub wasn't the only man who knew about it. *The Ideal Bartender* (1917) by Tom Bullock, a bartender from St. Louis, also detailed a Gibson Cocktail—again, sans onion—but he did call for a tad less dry vermouth (one ounce) than dry gin (one and a half ounces). The Dry Martini, even though it was masquerading under a different name, was still evolving.

"The Birth of the Gibson"

CHARLES DANA GIBSON, ILLUSTRATOR FOR MAGAZINES SUCH AS *LIFE* AND *HARPER'S*, WAS THE CREATOR OF THE GIBSON GIRL, HIS CONCEPT OF THE PERFECT AMERICAN WOMAN—TALL, AND BLESSED WITH OH-SO-LONG LEGS. GIBSON WAS ALSO A MEMBER OF NEW YORK'S PLAYERS CLUB, A GRAMERCY PARK ESTABLISHMENT FREQUENTED BY MANY STARS OF STAGE AND SCREEN, AND IT IS SAID THAT ON ONE EVENING, BEING BORED WITH HIS USUAL COCKTAIL, REQUESTED THAT BARTENDER, CHARLIE CONNOLLY, MIX HIM SOMETHING DIFFERENT. CONNOLLY ALLEGEDLY MIXED A DRY MARTINI AND GARNISHED IT WITH PEARL ONIONS, AND A NEW DRINK WAS BORN.

THERE HAVE BEEN STORIES PRINTED ABOUT A BUSINESS-MAN WHO WANTED TO STAY MORE SOBER THAN HIS COL-LEAGUES, AND HAD THE BARTENDER SERVE HIM WATER IN A COCKTAIL GLASS WITH PEARL ONIONS AS A GARNISH THAT WOULD ENSURE NOBODY MISTOOK HIS DRINK FOR THEIRS, BUT THE PLAYERS CLUB IN NEW YORK IS FAIRLY CERTAIN THAT THE GIBSON STORY BASED ON THEIR CLUB IS, INDEED, THE TRUE ONE.

During America's dry years—January 1920 to December 1933—many so-called Martinis were made with "bathtub" gin. The pure form of the drink, made from distilled London dry gin, continued to evolve on the other side of the Atlantic. According to *Cocktails and How to Mix Them,* by Robert Vermeire, a bartender at the Embassy Club in London and the American Bar in the Casino Municipal in Nice, France, European imbibers of the late 1920s who ordered a Martini were automatically presented with a drink made from dry gin and sweet vermouth. Other books from the same time period, however, differ. *An Anthology of Cocktails together with Selected Observations by a Distinguished Gathering and Diverse Thoughts for Great Occasions,* a promotional booklet published by Booth's gin, probably during the 1920s (the book isn't dated), detailed various Dry Martini recipes that called for equal parts dry gin and dry vermouth, and a couple of dashes of bitters—sometimes orange, sometimes Angostura.

Indeed, in 1926, *The Cocktail Book,* "issued for the St. Botolph Society by L. C. Page & Company, Boston," called for two parts dry gin to one part dry vermouth (and two dashes of orange bitters) in its recipe for the Dry Martini, and we can safely say that, even though Prohibition was in full force at the time, our beloved cocktail was almost recognizable as a Dry Martini. When Congress repealed the Volstead Act and Franklin Roosevelt declared that Prohibition was over in December 1933, American bartenders were as quick with their pens as they were with their shakers, and some interesting new cocktail books appeared on the shelves of post-Prohibition American bookstores.

One of the first new bartending guides to hit the scene was Patrick Gavin Duffy's *The Official Mixing Guide* (1934), and his recipe for "Martini Cocktail (dry)" contained two parts gin, one part French (dry) vermouth, and one dash of orange bitters. Two years later, Harman Burney Burke's *Complete Cocktail & Drinking Recipes* recommended the exact same ingredients and proportions. But very little mention was given, after the Noble Experiment, to Old Tom gin, and we must, therefore, presume that this peculiar product had lost its popularity (or distributor) by the 1930s. (Limited quantities of Old Tom gin are available but very hard to find. The product, however, is a compound, not distilled, gin.)

Even in 1947, when Trader Vic published his *Bartender's Guide,* the proportions for a Dry Martini remained at two parts gin to one part dry vermouth, but that practice would soon change—drastically. It seems

that sometime in the late 1940s or perhaps the early 1950s, vermouth began to be poured in shorter and shorter measures. David Embury's 1952 book, *The Fine Art of Mixing Drinks,* states, "Quite recently . . . there has sprung up the vermouth-rinse method of making Martinis. This consists of rinsing the inside surface of the cocktail glass with vermouth, pouring it back into the bottle, and then filling the glass with iced gin."

Embury didn't applaud this extra-dry version of what he called "the most perfect of apéritif cocktails." He preferred a seven to one gin to vermouth ratio and noted that a five to one Martini was acceptable for "even those who never before would drink a Martini." James Beard, the "Dean of American Cookery," concurred with Embury in his 1959 "revised and enlarged" version of Duffy's book—by then titled *The Standard Bartender's Guide*—in which Beard called for four or five measures of gin to each measure of dry vermouth.

By the mid-1960s, the *Old Mr. Boston De Luxe Official Bartender's Guide* included a whole section on the Martini. It claimed that popular proportions could range to an eight to one ratio of gin to vermouth and suggested that the reader use 80-proof gin (as opposed to the more popular 90-proof bottlings) to make a more traditional Dry Martini cocktail. The 1966 edition of this same guide actually included a chart to show that an eight to one Martini made with 90-proof gin will result in an 84-proof cocktail, whereas if it were made with 80-proof gin, the drink would be only 75.1 proof. Furthermore, the Martini section goes on to detail the Vodkatini (made with vodka instead of gin) and the tequila-based "Tequini" variation of the drink. Just where was the Dry Martini heading?

If you need historical precedence, you need look no further than Embury's book, in which he noted that Martinis could be made with gin, vodka, rum, or tequila, and also mentioned Martini variations that contained dashes of curaçao, crème de cassis, Chartreuse, or sherry. Truly, 1952 was half a century after the Martini was born, but still, Embury was known for being somewhat curmudgeonly when writing about new drinks, and it appears that he didn't bat an eyelash at these variations.

One group of wags, calling themselves the "American Standards Association," published the "American Standard Safety Code and Requirements for Dry Martinis" in 1966, and this document was obviously written by people who had a sense of humor but clearly didn't believe there was any room for Martini variations whatsoever. Included in the pages were such definitions as: "Lemonade. A term applied to drinks which have been subjected to the peel of a lemon. There is no place for the rind of any citrus fruit, or its oils, in an American Standard dry martini." Another entry is: "Vodka. A distilled alcoholic beverage made originally from potatoes, but now encountered in grain alcohol versions. It is never employed in a dry martini."

The document goes on

Pineapple Martinis

W. C. FIELDS, ONE OF THE WORLD'S MOST RENOWNED DRINKERS, IS SAID TO HAVE CARRIED A FLASK OF MARTINIS WHEN FILMING, BUT HE ALWAYS TOLD PEOPLE THAT THE FLASK WAS FULL OF PINEAPPLE JUICE. ONE DAY, SOMEBODY ON THE SET POURED FIELD'S MARTINIS AWAY AND FILLED THE FLASK WITH REAL PINEAPPLE JUICE, AND WHEN FIELDS TOOK A SLUG, HE IS SAID TO HAVE HOLLERED, "SOMEONE'S PUT PINEAPPLE JUICE IN MY PINEAPPLE JUICE!"

to note such things as the maximum olive size for a martini: .473 cubic inches for a $3\frac{1}{2}$-ounce cocktail—and on the subject of vermouth, it clearly states, "The employment of vermouth in an American Standard dry martini shall not be mandatory, provided no other ingredient is employed as a substitute." Finally, the work includes instructions on how to mix a Martini by "the radiation method," which involves placing a 60-watt light bulb exactly nine inches from a bottle of vermouth, and situating a bottle of gin twenty-three inches on the other side of the vermouth. By illuminating the bulb for a period of between seven and sixteen seconds ("Clear bottles require the shortest exposure"), it claimed that enough vermouth would be "radiated" into the gin to make an American Standard Dry Martini.

There are many Martini drinkers who would swear that the American Standards directives are holy, but the Martini continued to evolve. Many Martini variations appeared in the late 1960s and early 1970s, and the 1971 edition of *Playboy's Host and Bar Book* gives us some good examples of what had become acceptable by that time. Author Thomas Mario, *Playboy's* food and drink editor since 1953, had no qualms in noting forty-one Martini variations in his book, and some of them bore little or no resemblance to the classic Dry Martini cocktail. The Bloodhound, for instance, contained strawberry liqueur; the Matinée was made with sambuca, cream, and lime juice; and the Moldau was made from gin, rum, lime juice, pineapple juice, and sugar. True, Mario didn't call all of these variations "Martinis" per se, but he listed all of these drinks in the Martini section, calling them "variations on the familiar martini theme."

Today we are faced with two factions. Along with the current resurgence of classic cocktails have come many new drinks, and bartenders have called them Martinis whenever they want to add a touch of style to their newly created cocktails. Classicists, on the other hand, wail and moan at the thought of any drink being designated as a Martini unless it contains only dry vermouth and gin or vodka. What would these purists say if we suggested that a true Martini must have a couple of dashes of orange bitters—just the way the drink was made until the 1940s—and that a true classicist would insist on a drink made with, at most, two measures of gin to every tot of vermouth?

Though some will think this is a sad tale to have to tell, it's an undeniable fact that the Martini is no longer just a drink; the Martini is now a category of drinks—just like "sours," "slings," and "fizzes." If you merely order a "Martini" in one of today's new cocktail lounges, it's likely that you will be presented with a list as long as your arm that contains drinks that bear no resemblance to the Martinis of the 1940s and 1950s. However, you should not despair—the Dry Martini is still made with vermouth and gin, and the Dry Vodka Martini contains exactly the same ingredients as it ever has. And these drinks will continue to be hailed as the world's most glorious, most sophisticated, and most glamorous cocktails.

If you happen to be a staunch Martini purist, we should put your mind at ease by telling you up front that no more mention of Martini variations will enter this book until you come to the recipe section. And even there, we have gone to great lengths to choose only the most well-thought-out drinks to include in that particular chapter. We should also state, for the record, that without the purists of the world, drinks such as the classic Dry Martini might well have been lost in the post-Prohibition shuffle. As for us? We consider ourselves "progressive purists." When we order a Martini, we order a "Dry Gin (or Vodka) Martini," and when we want to sample Martini variations, we look to the menu and marvel at some of today's innovative upstarts.

"Martinis by the Bottle"

THOUGH PURISTS FROWN AT THE VERY THOUGHT OF IT, PRE-MIXED MARTINIS WERE AVAILABLE BY THE BOTTLE AS EARLY AS 1907. A PARK & TILFORD WHOLESALE WINE AND LIQUOR PRICE LIST PUBLISHED IN MARCH 1907, DETAILS HEUBLEIN'S CLUB COCKTAILS—MARTINIS AND MANHATTANS AMONG THEM—FOR SALE AT $10.50 PER DOZEN BOTTLES (PRESUMABLY QUARTS) OR $14.40 FOR 144 INDIVIDUAL BOTTLES. IN *THE BOOZE READER: A SOGGY SAGA OF A MAN IN HIS CUPS*, GEORGE BISHOP WROTE "THE (PRE-)PREPARED (MARTINI) IS USUALLY WATERED DOWN, OFTEN ON THE WARMISH SIDE, AND NOT VERY DRY; THREE CHARACTERISTICS THAT, IN A MARTINI, ARE ABOUT AS WELCOME AS SALTPETER IN A BORDELLO."

Gin

---ꞏⲟ/ⲟ/ⲟ/ⲟꞏ---

HOW AND WHEN WAS GIN CREATED? THIS most maligned of spirits, this "mother's ruin," this perfumed elixir that is said to have driven many to madness and some to genius, is often touted as the creation of a certain Franciscus de la Boë, aka Dr. Sylvius, a physician and professor at the University of Leyden, Holland, in the 1650s. But was the good doctor the very first to add the flavor of juniper to spirits? Probably not.

Hugh Williams, master distiller for United Distillers in London, theorizes that the twelfth-century alchemedic monks of Italy most likely were the first to use juniper to flavor some of the world's first spirits. Even though distillation equipment was used by Egyptian alchemists to make various elixirs, the Italian monks were almost certainly the first to produce beverage alcohol in the form of distilled spirits.

The juniper berry grew throughout Italy, and alchemists had recognized its diuretic qualities. During the

Bubonic Plague (1347–1350), records prove that distilled spirits were certainly used for medicinal purposes,
and it is believed that the Black Death did much to
acquaint the general populace with medicinal liquor.
Since the symptoms of the plague included the enlarge-
ment of lymph nodes, it follows that a diuretic, such as
juniper, would have been used to help reduce the swelling.
Did the alchemists infuse their spirits with juniper during
the plague? We simply don't know. The printing of books
did not become commonplace until more than a century
later, and the first mention of botanicals being used
in distillation dates to a book—*The vertuose Boke of
Distyllacyon of the Waters of all maner of Herbes*—published
in London in the 1520s. And so, although the theory of
an early form of gin existing since the mid-1300s, or
earlier, is entirely possible, it cannot be proved.

The "Dr. Sylvius" theory is a very confusing issue.
Our research has led us to various books on the subject
of spirits that refer to Sylvius creating gin in, or around
the year 1650. But some of these same volumes refer
to gin being known in England in the 1570s. And to
add to the confusion, in *A History of Vodka* (of all
places), William Pokhlebkin states that in 1485 "the
first English gin (was) prepared at the court of Henry
VII." We have been unable to verify Pokhlebkin's state-

ment, but it does seem very likely that gin was made in Holland during the 1500s, long before Sylvius wrote the first known printed recipe for the spirit. It should be mentioned, however, that some historians contend that the Sylvius recipe was the first to contain grain-based spirits, whereas earlier juniper-flavored liquors were distilled from fruits—most likely grapes.

In 1568, the predominately Protestant Dutch revolted against their Catholic rulers from Spain, and in 1585 Queen Elizabeth I of England sent Robert Dudley, Earl of Leicester, to help the Dutch in their quest. Dudley's soldiers did more than fight, however; they discovered *jenever*—the Dutch name of a juniper-flavored spirit—and they praised it because it had given them "Dutch Courage" before battles. The French word for juniper is *genièvre*, and although gin was initially known as "Hollands," the English eventually shortened either the Dutch or French word for juniper and anglicized it until it became "gin."

The port cities of England—Bristol, Plymouth, Portsmouth, and London—started to produce their own gins in the early 1600s, and according to John Doxat's *Book of Drinking*, by 1688, England was producing a half-million gallons of gin per year. The following year, William III (a Dutchman descended from Charles I of

England) succeeded to the British throne with his wife, Queen Mary, and decided to try to increase that figure.

The Protestant William attempted to curtail Catholic France's economy while at the same time boosting England's. He banned the importation of anything at all from France, thus forcing English farmers to use more homegrown grains to make spirits. Gin soon started to pour out of many a still in the green and pleasant land, because although the English could survive without French brandy, they did need a replacement. Furthermore, Queen Anne, who succeeded William in 1702, canceled the "Distiller's Charter," effectively making it legal for any Tom, Dick, or Harry to make his own gin. This gave birth to a rhyme:

The Quack Vintners

So Quacks, for Cordials, filthy spirits sell,
Which soon despatch the sick to Heaven or Hell,
Not caring whether they are bless'd or curs'd,
Since they have pick'd the Patient's Pocket first.

By 1727, the approximately six million English folk were drinking five million gallons of gin per year, and the government was somewhat distressed by the daily drunkenness of its citizens. According to André Simon in his wonderful tome entitled *Drink,* a work was published in 1733 that described spirits as "the masterpiece of the devil," and went on to say, "Physicians observe that these distilled spirituous liquors, which are inflamed by repeated distillation, are, in a manner, direct poison to human bodies." In 1736, Parliament sought to quell the problem by introducing the Gin Act, which proclaimed it illegal to sell gin in quantities of less than two gallons, and required a £50 license fee for anyone desirous of distilling gin for sale. The Gin Act constituted an obvious move to keep gin out of the hands of the common folk, who could never afford to buy a full two gallons of gin at once. At first glance, this act might seem like a government's concern for its citizens, but nothing could be farther from the truth. In fact, the upper classes were merely worried that their "inferiors" weren't getting enough work done. But gin distilling continued—in homes as well as in distilleries—and the law was circumvented by calling their product "Parliamentary Brandy" or anything at all—except gin. By 1743, gin production had soared to 20 million gallons, and it has been estimated that, on average, each Londoner of that time was downing almost eighteen ounces of gin each day. The Gin Act, unreasonable and unenforceable, was repealed that same year and replaced in 1751 by a more palatable tax structure.

So drunk were the Londoners of the time that, during the mid-1700s, plays had to be canceled because the audiences were too befuddled to sit still, and the actors were too drunk to remember their lines. By the middle of the century, ruination at the hands of gin had become so commonplace that artist William Hogarth put his hand to *Gin Lane*, a street scene depicting the gin-induced horrors of the time. In *Drinks of the World* (1892), authors James Mew and John Aston say, "Hogarth tells us that in Gin Lane every circumstance of the horrid effects of gin drinking is brought to view *in terrorem*," and they go on to include a poem written by a certain Reverend James Townley to commemorate Hogarth's art:

Martini drinkers of the stage and screen

HUMPHREY BOGART

LUIS BUÑUEL

GEORGE BURNS

JOHNNY CARSON

MARGO CHANNING

MARLENE DIETRICH

W. C. FIELDS

AVA GARDNER

CARY GRANT

WILLIAM HOLDEN

DEBORAH KERR

JACK LEMMON

DEAN MARTIN

TYRONE POWER

FRANK SINATRA

BILLY WILDER

Gin Lane

Gin, cursed fiend, with fury fraught,
Makes human race a prey;
It enters by a deadly draught,
And steals our life away.
Virtue and Truth, driven to despair,
Its rage compels to fly;
But cherishes, with hellish care,
Theft, murder, perjury.
Damned cup, that on the vitals preys,
That liquid fire contains;
Which madness to the heart conveys,
And rolls it through the veins.

———

Most, if not all, gins made in the mid-1700s were sweetened with sugar in an attempt to mask the off flavors of badly made products, and this style of gin became known as "Old Tom." The name usually is credited to a certain Captain Dudley Bradstreet, who was a government agent who tattled on illicit distillers and was himself a purveyor of gin in London. In his book, *The Life and Uncommon Adventures of Captain Dudley Bradstreet* (1755), Bradstreet described exactly his method for selling small quantities of gin during the time when the Gin Act required minimum quantities of at least two gallons: "I . . . purchased in Moorfields the sign of a cat and had it nailed to a street window. I then caused a leaden pipe, the small end out about an inch, to be placed under the paw of the cat, the end that was within had a funnel to it. . . . When the liquor was properly disposed, I got a person to inform a few of the mob that gin would be sold by the cat at my window next day, provided they put money in his mouth . . . at last I heard the chink of money and a comfortable voice say, 'Puss, give me two pennyworth of gin!' I instantly put my mouth to the tube and bid them receive it from the pipe under her paw." It should be noted that, within Bradstreet's text, he refers to the cat as both "him" and "her," but nevertheless, after a few days, Bradstreet claimed to be making good money—£3 to £4 a day—in return for his gin, and the term "Old Tom" is said to have been derived from this, probably the world's first vending machine.

In Britain, the Industrial Revolution began in the late 1700s. It was also around this time that the Gin Palaces of England started to appear—a fact that the growing temperance movement in Britain despised. Gin palaces were ornate, fancy pubs where the working man and woman could drink themselves into oblivion, trying to forget their squalid living conditions. In his 1836 work, *Sketches by Boz,* Charles Dickens had this to say about the state of the gin-swilling nation: "Gin drinking is a great vice in England, but wretchedness and dirt are greater; and until you improve the homes of the poor, or persuade a half-famished wretch not to seek relief in the temporary oblivion of his own misery, with the pittance which, divided among his family, would furnish a morsel of bread for each, gin-shops will increase in number and splendour. If Temperance Societies would suggest an antidote for hunger, filth, and foul air, or could establish dispensaries for the gratuitous distribution of bottles of Lethe-water, gin-palaces would be numbered among the things that were."

In *Stirred-Not Shaken: The Dry Martini,* author John Doxat states that by the mid-Victorian era, gin had become the drink of upper-crust English ladies, and in true Victorian fashion, they referred to it as "white wine." Not only did these people refuse to utter the word "gin," they actually reversed the letters and kept it in decanters labeled "nig." But things were about to change for gin, and dry gin, as opposed to the sweetened "Old

Tom" variety, appeared on the market sometime in the 1870s. This gin, according to *The World Guide to Spirits, Aperitifs and Cocktails* by Tony Lord, was advertised as "unsweetened," and, of course, this is the style of gin that we favor today in our Martinis.

Dry gin was probably a result of new distillation techniques that produced better-quality spirits that didn't have faults that needed to be masked with sugar. The invention of the continuous still in the 1830s certainly played a part in the increased purity of distilled spirits, and in the cases of gin and vodka, this new type of still was a massive advantage to distillers and consumers alike. Vodka needs to be flavorless, and gin distillers need, basically, very pure vodka to redistill along with their carefully chosen botanicals.

Gin has long been popular in the United States, as evidenced by Jerry Thomas, famed nineteenth-century bartender who detailed eighteen gin-based drinks in the first edition (1862) of his book, *How to Mix Drinks*. But

A "Different" Martini-Making Technique:

DRINK A LITTLE VERMOUTH.

EXHALE INTO THE BOWL OF A CHILLED MARTINI GLASS.

FILL THE GLASS WITH GIN.

the Old Tom sweetened gins remained, to a certain extent, quite popular in this country until the turn of the century, when, according to *Stirred-Not Shaken,* wealthy Americans traveling to Europe returned to the States with a newfound fondness for London dry gin. Still, until that dark day in 1920 when American bars closed for the Noble Experiment that seemed to last an eternity, Old Tom gin remained somewhat popular. And when the taverns reopened their doors in December 1933, American bartenders found that the public at large had become more and more enamored of dry gin. Old Tom was on its way out.

Although gin was commonplace and quite popular before Prohibition, whiskey was the public's favorite spirit. When whiskey became hard to come by—and rather expensive when it was available—homemade, or bathtub, gin became the drink of choice. This product was easy to make but poor—very poor—in quality. John Hilgert, a bartender in a Prohibition-era speakeasy in Ohio, remembers watching his boss prepare gin by simply mixing grain alcohol, distilled water, and juniper flavoring—and this all occurred in the basement of the club. Distilled dry gin has the flavorings distilled into the spirit, and the "bathtub" gin, now known as "compound gin," that was so popular during Prohibition, is not nearly as complex and aromatic. However, this illicit product gave Americans a taste for gin such as they had never had before, and the Martini-crazed sophisticates of the 1940s and 1950s owed their love of gin, in large part, to Prohibition.

Perhaps the most incredible fact about gin is that, throughout history, it has been a maligned spirit, declared to be responsible for sin and degradation in the eighteenth and nineteenth centuries, and perhaps the most common illicit product during America's almost-fourteen-year ban on beverage alcohol. And yet, gin has emerged as one of the world's most desirable spirits. Maybe the gin distillers owe much to the creation of the Dry Martini. After all, what could be more desirable than producing the main ingredient of the world's most sophisticated drink?

How Gin Is Made

Juniper, of course, is always the primary flavoring agent in gin, but how the essence of the juniper gets into the gin is a rather complicated story. Every major distillery has its own idiosyncratic techniques for making what each claims to be the best gin on the market. Juniper isn't the only flavoring used; many others are added to most gins. Coriander and angelica are often used as the secondary spices, but other botanicals, such as fennel, calamus root, cardamom, cassia, ginger, cinnamon, licorice, caraway seed, and citrus peels, are commonly added to gin. Most distillers will never divulge their complete list of botanicals, but although a few will tell you exactly which herbs and spices they use, the specific amounts

> INTO A MIXING GLASS FULL OF ICE POUR AT LEAST A QUARTER BOTTLE OF DRY GIN, STIR AND STRAIN INTO TWO LARGE GOBLETS. ADD— TWO PUFFS FROM A SCENT SPRAY CONTAINING FRENCH VERMOUTH, I WATCHED THIS BEING MIXED BY A FRIEND IN NEW YORK, WHEN I GENTLY REMONSTRATED, HE SAID "GEE, CEDRIC, THIS ONE IS IN YOUR HONOUR; I USUALLY PASS THE CORK OVER THE GLASS!"
>
> CEDRIC DICKENS
> (GREAT-GRANDSON OF
> CHARLES DICKENS)

of those botanicals are never revealed. It's a secret. And we should take time to thank the gods of the juniper berries that such secrets exist—we all need a little mystery in our lives.

So how do we know which gin is the best gin? It really amounts to personal preference. Some of us like the juniper to sing on through our gin, with the other botanicals taking a backseat, and others prefer the fragrant scent of lemon zest, coriander, or angelica to join the juniper up front. Whose distillation techniques are the best? Once again, it's up to the individual to judge. All we know is that these techniques are usually very precise and time-consuming and that no profit-seeking company would go to such lengths if they believed a suitable shortcut existed.

All gins start their lives as neutral spirits, basically a high-proof vodka that runs out of a continuous still at a minimum of 190 proof, or ninety-five percent alcohol, and these spirits are often made at one distillery and then shipped to a separate facility where they are redistilled with the botanicals and become gin. Legally, the spirits can be made from any agricultural product whatsoever—grapes, sugar, potatoes, beets, you name it—but most gins are distilled from grain.

It is also legal to take these neutral grain spirits, add oils or essences of juniper and other botanicals, dilute the mixture with demineralized water to bottling proof (not less than 40 percent alcohol), and call it "gin." Thus, our first bit of advice concerning gin: If the label doesn't include the word "distilled" or the designation "London dry," don't buy it. This product is probably "compound" gin, made with the flavorings stirred in, rather than fresh botanicals actively distilled into the spirit.

"London dry" gin is yet another source of confusion in the gin game—it doesn't have to be made in England, let alone London town, to be called "London dry." The term describes a *style* of gin created in London in the

late 1800s. London dry gin must be distilled gin, and like all other gins, juniper must be the predominant flavor.

Plymouth gin has a style similar to London dry, but it, like all of the other distilled gins, is made to the company's own recipe and techniques, and as such, is different from all others. It must however, be distilled in Plymouth, England, and only one company—Coates— produces Plymouth gin. At the time of writing no Plymouth gin is available in the United States, but the Coates distillery is currently trying to arrange to export their gin to us. Hopefully, by the time you read this, Plymouth gin will be in your liquor store.

Production

Although the master distillers regulate the production of their neutral spirits, the real job begins after the spirit has been tested to make sure that it is as free from flavor as possible. After the spirit is found acceptable, the botanicals will be added. However, at most distilleries, the botanicals themselves go through a rigorous selection process, and this is part of the master distiller's craft.

Each gin-maker reviews hundreds of samples of botanicals, yet few are selected. Only the very best are purchased, and then they are stored under very specific conditions until deemed ready for distilling into the gin. At this stage,

Importers, pulled out all the stops trying to convince International Distillers and Vintners, his parent company in London, that they needed to extend their line of Bombay gin. "For a whole year they refused to go ahead with the concept," recalls Roux, "but then, just before a major executive left the company, he told me to bypass everyone else and go ahead with the project. It was his parting gift to me." Once again, Bombay gin, this time in a gorgeous blue bottle and bearing the name "Sapphire," was a huge hit.

Production

The Bombay bottlings actually display the botanicals used to make each one: The regular bottling utilizes coriander seeds from Morocco, licorice from China, lemon peel and almonds from Spain, angelica from Saxony, orris (iris root) and juniper berries from Italy, and cassia bark from Indochina. Bombay Sapphire incorporates all of these same botanicals but adds cubeb berries from Java and grains of paradise from West Africa to differentiate the recipe. Although juniper is, as it must be, the predominant botanical used, the company asserts that it doesn't use as much juniper as most other gins and claims that this results in a smoother product.

Both bottlings of Bombay gin are produced from neutral spirits redistilled with the botanicals, but the method differs from others inasmuch as the vapors from the pot still (and this company uses a type of still known as a "Carter Head Still" fitted with a tall vertical column) are funneled into a copper basket that holds the botanicals. "It's akin to steaming vegetables instead of boiling them," says a spokesperson for the company.

Tasting Notes

Bombay
Spicy floral nose with soft waft of juniper; medium body, fruity palate with a juniper backdrop, long finish. Recommended.

Bombay Sapphire
Spicier nose than the regular Bombay—juniper and coriander; medium body, crisp and spicy palate, juniper peeks through spicy backdrop; long, crisp finish. Recommended.

Boodles British Gin
Made in Britain, 45.2% alcohol by volume

Boodles is a product of Joseph E. Seagram & Sons, and unfortunately nothing is known about the history of the product, except "Cock-Russell & Co. Ltd., Established 1845," which appears on the label. Although the word "distilled" does not appear on the Boodles label, the words "London Dry Gin" tell us that this is, indeed, a distilled gin. Boodles is distilled under pressure, thus allowing the alcohol to evaporate at a lower temperature, and preserving the fresh flavors of the botanicals.

Tasting Notes

Soft floral nose with juniper high notes; wonderfully balanced palate—juniper up front with complex floral backdrop; crisp, clean finish with lingering juniper. Highly recommended.

Booth's Distilled London Dry Gin
Made in the U.S., 45% alcohol by volume

Booth's, a company established in 1740, proudly emblazons its labels with a royal crest and the words "by appointment to Her Majesty the Queen." According to *The Kindred Spirit—A History of Gin and the House of Booth* by Lord Kinross, although many Booths are known to have been in the wine and spirits business in the 1700s—one as early as 1716—it wasn't until 1778 that the firm of Phillip Booth & Company had grown large enough to be included in the *Directory of Merchants* as owners of a distillery. Although it isn't known which member of the Booth family operated the distillery to which the label's "1740" date refers, Kinross asserts that the business definitely existed.

After Phillip Booth's death in 1818, his son, Felix, succeeded him and took the company to new heights. He built a new distillery in Brentford, a port on the River Thames, bought a nearby brewery, and built a hotel on the adjacent land. On the fields surrounding his facilities

FELIX BOOTH, SON OF THE FOUNDER OF BOOTH'S GIN, WAS A VERY PROMINENT CITIZEN IN NINETEENTH-CENTURY ENGLAND. IN 1828, HE WAS ELECTED A SHERIFF OF THE CITY OF LONDON, AND THE FOLLOWING YEAR, HAVING AMASSED A SIZEABLE FORTUNE FROM HIS GIN BUSINESS, HE FINANCED A VOYAGE TO FIND THE NORTHWEST PASSAGE. ALTHOUGH THE EXPEDITION FAILED IN ITS PRIMARY PURPOSE, IT RESULTED IN FELIX BOOTH'S NAME BEING HONORED WHEN CAPTAIN JOHN ROSS NAMED FELIX HARBOR AND THE BOOTHIA PENINSULA (NORTHEAST OF KING WILLIAM ISLAND, CANADA). IT WAS ON THAT VOYAGE THAT THE CAPTAIN'S NEPHEW, JAMES CLARK ROSS, ESTABLISHED THE TRUE POSITION OF THE MAGNETIC NORTH POLE, HE IS SAID TO HAVE CELEBRATED THE DISCOVERY BY PLANTING A UNION JACK AND TOASTING FELIX BOOTH WITH A TOT OF BOOTH'S GIN.

POINTING NORTH
COURTESY OF BOOTH'S GIN

Felix grew corn, which he used to make his gin, and kept cattle that were fed on the leftovers from the distilling process. This was the largest distilling business in all England. Felix died, a childless bachelor, in 1850, and the company passed into the hands of distant relatives.

Production

Today, Booth's Gin is owned by United Distillers, which also owns the Gordon's and Tanqueray brands. According to Hugh Williams, Master Distiller for U.D. in England, each of the three products uses different recipes for its botanicals. All of them, though, share the same method for introducing the juniper, coriander, angelica, and other secret ingredients to the neutral spirit immediately before distillation in a pot still. Williams, a man who strongly believes that if the botanicals are allowed to steep in the spirit before distillation the resultant gin will bear a "stewed" nose, also asserts that the recipe for Booth's is the same one that has been used since the 1700s, and the pot still is an exact replica of the one used by Felix Booth.

Tasting Notes

Soft juniper nose; medium body; wonderful perfumed palate with juniper right up front of floral/coriander backdrop; crisp, dry finish. Recommended.

Bradburn's Sequentially Distilled English Gin

Made in England, 47.4% alcohol by volume

Little is known of the history of Bradburn's gin, though the distillers claim that their recipe dates to the 1850s. Most interesting, however, is the unusual method used for making it. While most gins distill all of their botanicals into the spirit at once, Bradburn's is made in three separate distillations, each one at a different temperature and using different ingredients. The company's purpose for all this extra effort is "to derive optimum flavor from each individual botanical ingredient." Finally, the three separate distillates are married to produce Bradburn's gin.

Tasting Notes

Sweetish fruity nose; medium body;
sweet herbal/floral/fruity palate with mostly hidden
juniper notes; long finish.

Sir Robert Burnett's Distilled London Dry Gin

Made in the U.S., 40% alcohol by volume

Burnett's Crown Select Distilled London Dry Gin

Made in England, 47% alcohol by volume

Unfortunately, most of the history pertaining to these brands has been lost. However, Stephen Bayley refers to Sir Robert Burnett in his book, *Gin,* which claims that in 1770, Mr. Burnett joined a company that had been in existence since 1679, and in time bought the company and named it after himself. Burnett was made a Sheriff of London in 1794 and was knighted the following year.

Production

Heaven Hill Distilleries, the present owners of Burnett's gin, states that the spirit still is made to its original formula, and although the higher-proof Crown Select bottling is made in England, the company went to the trouble of bringing an English gin distiller to the United States in order to learn how to make the American-made product as authentic as possible.

Burnett's gin is different from most in that it uses a method of vacuum distillation that causes the alcohol to evaporate at a lower temperature. Therefore, since the botanicals are added to the neutral spirit prior to distillation, they are "warmed," rather than boiled. Heaven

Hill also attributes the distinctive flavor of this gin to a "superior form of angelica found by Sir Robert Burnett in a remote corner of Turkey."

Tasting Notes

Burnett's

High citrus notes in the nose; light body with citrus palate hiding most juniper notes; short finish.

Burnett's Crown Select

Perfumed juniper nose; soft body; nicely balanced juniper palate with floral/fruity notes; medium-long finish. Recommended.

Calvert Distilled London Dry Gin

Made in the U.S., 40% alcohol by volume

Here's a true-blue American London Dry Gin named for the family descended from George Calvert, the first Lord Baltimore. In 1632, the year of his death, Calvert received a land grant from Charles I of England that encompassed what is now Maryland and parts of Delaware and Pennsylvania. George Calvert didn't live to enjoy his colony, but his sons created a place of religious freedom and the first colony that admitted foreigners as citizens. The Calvert family's dispute with the Penns of Pennsylvania led to the establishment of the Mason-Dixon Line in the 1760s, and in the nineteenth century, Calverts founded the Calvert-Maryland Distilling Company.

Production

The Jim Beam Brands Company, owners of Calvert gin, is unable to reveal anything about their gin distillation process other than that it is "distilled from the finest grain neutral spirits and carries the flavor of the finest botanicals."

Tasting Notes

Simple, citrusy nose; medium body;
citrus palate with some sour notes; short, hot finish.

Coates Distilled Plymouth Dry Gin
Made in Plymouth, England,
47% alcohol by volume

Author's note: At the time of writing, Plymouth Gin was not available in the United States. In 1996, a small group of

*enthusiastic entrepreneurs took over this label and the dis-
tillery, and if all goes according to plan, by the time you are
reading this you will be able to sample this fine product. The
tasting notes pertain to a sample of Plymouth gin at 47%
alcohol by volume, the proof at which the company is plan-
ning to release the gin in the United States.*

In the early 1600s, gin was being made in all of south-
ern England's major ports—Bristol, Portsmouth,
Plymouth, and London. Each port is said to have produced its own style of gin, and much as we'd like to compare all four, only the London and Plymouth styles have
survived into the twentieth century. Unlike London gin,
Plymouth gin is the only one that must be made within
the geographical confines of the city it represents.
Indeed, in the late nineteenth century, the Coates family
successfully lobbied to prevent anyone outside Plymouth
from using that designation on their gin.

Plymouth gin has been made at the Black Friars
Distillery in Plymouth, England, since 1793, and parts
of this building have been in use since 1425, when the
Black Friar monks inhabited it as a monastery. It is said
that the Pilgrim fathers slept in the monastery before
departing for what became Plymouth Rock. Another historical note of interest is that Sir Francis Drake designed

the leat (duct) that brings water from
Dartmoor into Plymouth—the same
water used to make Plymouth gin.

As a major port, the city supplied
many ships of the Royal Navy with
Plymouth gin (among other things) and
therefore it has always been known as the
"official" gin of the Royal Navy. The creation
of the cocktail Pink Gin, or "Pinkers"
(gin and Angostura bitters), is said to have
originated with British Navy officers who
took bitters to cure what ailed them, and added
Plymouth gin to make the drink more palatable.

Production

The manager of the Black Friars Distillery is Sean
Harrison, an ex-Royal Navy man—who better to make
this gin? Harrison tells us that, although the botanicals
used to make Plymouth gin are the exact same ones the
original recipe called for—juniper berries, coriander,
angelica, orris, cardamom, and peels from oranges and
lemons—the proportions were altered slightly in the
1920s and resulted in a drier gin than the previous product. He adds that it is the use of orris and cardamom, and
the absence of heavier botanicals such as cinnamon, that

makes this a lighter, fruitier gin, without the heavy "bottom notes" found in some London dry gins.

The distillery still uses water from the moors of Dartmoor, both to dilute the neutral spirit before distillation and to bring the gin down to bottle proof before bottling. They use a 100-year-old pot still and the botanicals are added immediately before distillation—a practice common to the distillery since its eighteenth-century origins.

Tasting Notes

Dry juniper nose with fresh herbal backdrop;
body; highly perfumed, very dry palate with complex fresh
juniper/herbal/floral notes; crisp, dry finish.
Highly recommended.

Corney & Barrow Imported London Distilled Dry Gin

Made in the United Kingdom,
47.3% alcohol by volume

The Corney family has been in the beverage alcohol business in England since 1780, when Edward Bland Corney opened a small wine shop in London. He died in

1833 and the company was taken over by his son, Thomas, who took a cousin, Robert Phillipson Barrow, as a partner some five years later. The company holds Royal Warrants from King George V; Charles, the Prince of Wales; and Her Majesty Queen Elizabeth, the Queen Mother.

Tasting Notes

Crisp, complex, citrus/juniper nose; thick, supple body with highly complex juniper-perfumed palate—very well balanced with some citrus notes; crisp, clean finish with lingering complexity. Highly recommended.

Gilbey's Distilled London Dry Gin
Made in the U.S., 40% alcohol by volume

Two veterans of the Crimean War went into the wine business in London around 1860. These brothers, Walter and Alfred Gilbey, went from strength to strength and, in the 1870s, built their own distillery. The company met with continued success and license to make Gilbey's gin in America was granted in 1938. The brand is now owned in the United States by the Jim Beam Brands Company.

Production

The production processes used to make Gilbey's gin are a closely guarded secret, but the company does reveal that it uses juniper berries from Bavaria, orange peels from Spain, and "other rare herbs from around the world." The Jim Beam Brands Company also asserts that the formula for making Gilbey's gin is "unique in that its secret 'filter' results in a distinctive, carefully balanced flavor that is clean and fresh."

Tasting Notes

Dry, juniper nose; medium body; crisp palate with nice balance of juniper and citrus; crisp, lingering finish. Recommended.

Gordon's Distilled London Dry Gin

Made in the U.S., 40% alcohol by volume

Alexander Gordon, son of George Gordon of Aberdeen, was born in 1742, and according to an article in a 1907 edition of the *Huntly Express* by J. M. Bulloch, by 1783, Gordon and Company was a registered distiller in Southwark, England. Other papers, however, suggest that Gordon had been making gin as early as 1774, when he was described as a distiller on his daughter's birth certificate, and still other accounts pinpoint 1769 as the year in which Gordon started to make gin. Whatever the year, it is generally recognized that this man was one of the very first gin producers to make the dry style of gin that we use in our Martinis today, and this was no small feat.

Before dry gin was created, most drinkable gins were sweetened with sugar, mainly to mask the flavors of poorly made spirits. In order to produce dry gin, the distiller had to go to extraordinary measures to make sure that the solids in the distiller's mash didn't scorch or

JULIA CHILD, THE DOYENNE OF FINE COOKING, ENJOYS AN OCCASIONAL MARTINI, BUT CONFESSES THAT ONE IS HER LIMIT: "ONE OF MY FIRST MARTINIS WAS PROBABLY WHEN I WAS IN BOARDING SCHOOL IN CALIFORNIA," SHE RECALLS, "MY ROOMMATE HAD A COUPLE OF UNCLES WHO LIVED NEARBY, AND THEY WOULD GO THROUGH TREMENDOUS RITUAL TO MAKE THEIR MARTINIS. MY FRIEND AND I WERE ALLOWED ONLY ONE EACH, HOWEVER." A FAVORED DRINK OF MS. CHILD'S IS WHAT SHE CALLS "THE REVERSE MARTINI." SHE TAKES A LARGE, LONG-STEMMED WINE GLASS, FILLS IT WITH ICE, AND POURS IN NOILLY PRAT VERMOUTH TO REACH ABOUT HALF AN INCH FROM THE TOP. THEN JULIA POURS IN A LITTLE TOT OF GIN ("I REALLY LIKE GORDON'S GIN, AND IT'S NOT TOO EXPENSIVE.") SO THAT IT FLOATS ON TOP, "I CAN DRINK TWO OF THOSE," SHE BOASTS.

burn during distillation and thus impart a burned flavor to the gin. Without this off-flavor, sugar wasn't needed to disguise the gin. Before the invention of the continuous still in the 1830s (see page 101) controlling the temperature of the coal-fired pot stills required skill, patience, and determination.

In time, Alexander's son, Charles Gordon, joined the company, and although they had a few partners along the way, it was a merchant banker by the name of Currie who took over the company in 1892, and six years later amalgamated Gordon's with the Tanqueray gin distilling company.

Production

A representative of United Distillers in England told us that the recipe for Gordon's gin is the same one that has been used since the 1700s, and the pot stills are exact replicas of a 1780 still that was nicknamed "Old Tom." The original Old Tom was used by Alexander Gordon himself, and still is in use today. Although the company told us that juniper berries, coriander, and angelica are all used in the production of Gordon's, the other botanicals remain secret. We were told, however, that the botanicals are added to the spirit immediately prior to distillation; they are not allowed to steep in the spirit—a method used by some other gin distillers.

Tasting Notes

Crisp, juniper nose, nicely balanced with coriander;
medium body with strong juniper notes balanced well
with citrus/spice backdrop; medium, spicy finish.
Recommended.

Seagram's Distilled Extra Dry Gin
Made in the U.S., 40% alcohol by volume

The history of the company Joseph E. Seagram & Sons, starts in 1857 on a farm in Canada, when Joseph E. Seagram built a distillery in order to make whiskey from his surplus grains. Seagram's gin, however, wasn't introduced until 1939, when it was offered as "Seagram's Ancient Bottle Distilled Dry Gin." The original bottle was textured with sea shells and starfish, and even today, Seagram's gin comes in a textured bottle and is sometimes marketed as "The Smooth Gin in the Bumpy Bottle."

Production

The exact recipe for the botanicals used in Seagram's gin is, of course, a secret, but the company does state that juniper berries from Italy, cardamom from Sri Lanka, cassia bark from Vietnam, orange peel from Spain, coriander seeds from the Czech Republic, and angelica root from Germany are all included in the recipe.

This gin is distilled under pressure, a practice that a spokesperson for the company maintains helps preserve the natural flavors of the botanicals. In addition, the Seagram company ages the product in oak casks for about three months before the gin is bottled—a very rare occurrence in the gin industry. Due to federal regulations, neither gins nor vodkas are allowed to be labeled as "aged," but if you note the pale yellow color of this gin, and take note of the word "mellowed" on the label, you will have evidence of its having spent time in the wood.

Tasting Notes

Soft, subtle nose; soft body;
well-balanced herbal/spicy palate, not a lot of juniper;
short finish. Good choice for those who don't favor
highly floral, "strong" gins.

Squire's London Dry Gin
Made in England, 47% alcohol by volume

The Pope family of England own Squire's gin, and they named the product for their ancestor, Thomas Pope

(1721-1797), who they say was a "typical squire in the beautiful county of Dorset."

Production

According to the company, Squire's is a grain-based gin distilled "by the pot-still method . . . with the original recipe of botanicals, spices, and fruits."

Tasting Notes

Light floral nose; soft body; fruity,
almost sweet, palate; short finish.

Original Schlichte Steinhäger
Made in Germany, 38% alcohol by volume

Technically, this spirit is not classified as a gin, but as a "Steinhäger," a juniper-based spirit reputed to have originated in the village of Steinhagen, Germany, during the fifteenth century. In 1688, the Prussian Sovereign issued a decree allowing distillers to make this spirit commercially, and the company that makes this product, Schlichte, was founded in 1766. Steinhäger, according to EEC regulations, can be made only in the village of Steinhagen.

Production

Schlichte Steinhäger is a triple-distilled grain spirit flavored by juniper berries only and reduced to bottling
proof by spring water. (German law doesn't allow any
botanicals other than juniper to be used in the production of this spirit.)

Tasting Notes

*Heavy, malty nose; medium body; very subtle palate with
malt sweetness and very little juniper (even though it's the
only botanical they use); medium finish.*

Tanqueray Special Dry Distilled English Gin
Made in England, 47.3% alcohol by volume

The Tanqueray company was founded in 1830 when
Charles Tanqueray, a descendant of David Tanqueray, a
silversmith to the British royal family, perfected a recipe
of botanicals and became a gin distiller. He used the
waters from Finsbury Spa, just outside London, to make
his gin, and it is said that Daniel Defoe, Guy Fawkes,
and Nell Gwynn all took Finsbury waters for its
restorative powers. When Charles died in 1868, his

son, Charles Waugh Tanqueray, replaced him as head of the company, and in 1898, Tanqueray was amalgamated with the Gordon's gin distillery.

The bottle used for Tanqueray gin is said to have been modeled on an eighteenth-century British fire hydrant, but other accounts from the company state that the bottle was meant to suggest a cocktail shaker.

Production

A spokesperson for Charles Tanqueray & Company in London asserts that the recipe for Tanqueray gin is the same one that was developed by Charles Tanqueray in 1830 and that the pot still used today is an exact replica of the one used by Charles himself. Although the gin is made with juniper berries, coriander, and angelica in the botanicals, the other ingredients remain a closely guarded secret. However, the Tanqueray gin distillery insists that the botanicals be added to the spirit immediately prior to distillation, no steeping time allowed.

Tasting Notes

Fresh, herbal, very dry nose; medium yet dry body;
very complex herbal/floral/spicy palate with juniper right up
front; crisp, dry finish that lingers a long time.
Highly recommended.

Vodka

———⟨◦/◦/◦⟩———

IT'S HARD TO IMAGINE THAT VODKA—CLEAR
as a mountain stream, virtually odorless, and with a
taste that relies more on texture than flavor to distin-
guish one bottling from another—could be the source of
very much controversy. However, in the late 1970s,
when the Soviet Union boosted exports of its native
drink to the West, certain distillers in Poland took note.
About a decade later Poland took a stand on the issue,
claiming that vodka had been made in their country
before it ever was heard of in Russia and demanding that
they be allowed to decide who could use the term
"vodka." Just as Scotch whisky, by international agree-
ment, can be made only in Scotland, the proud people of
Poland wanted exclusive rights to the word "vodka."

Was vodka created by the Russians or the Poles?
To some extent, the question is tied to the birth of dis-
tilled spirits as a whole. According to "The Historical
Development of Distilling Plant," a paper written by

> I ALWAYS CARRY A
> REASONABLE AMOUNT OF
> MEDICINAL STIMULANTS
> IN CASE I ENCOUNTER A
> VENOMOUS SNAKE—WHICH
> I ALSO KEEP ON HAND.
>
> W. C. FIELDS

A. J. V. Underwood, D.Sc., F.I.C., in 1935, although ancient alchemists used stills to make various medicines and perfumes, it probably wasn't until the century between 1050 and 1150 that the first imbibable distilled spirits, probably made from wine, were produced.

Spirits were known by a number of names by the alchemedic monks who first produced them. Initially they were called "ardent waters," because of their ability to be ignited ("ardent" is derived from the Latin *ardere* meaning "to burn"), and eventually spirits became known as "the water of life," translated into a number of languages as *eau-de-vie, aquavit,* and, to some extent, vodka. Literally translated, vodka is a diminutive of the Russian word *voda,* meaning "water," but William Pokhlebkin, author of *A History of Vodka,* points out that by sometime around the middle of the thirteenth century, the word *voda* was used in legends as a symbol of life, and therefore we can infer that by the time *vodka* was used in Russia to describe distilled liquor, *vodka* meant "water of life." It's easy to understand why some people thought that spirits could hold a key to longevity. The syllogism they formulated was simple: If wine made you feel good, and distilled wine made you feel good faster, then there must be something in there that restores health.

Another somewhat amusing story about how vodka got its name was told to us some years ago by Mark Fish, a man who had worked as a plant manager at the Moscow Liquor and Vodka Plant (one of the distilleries that produces Stolichnaya). Fish tells of the day when he was doing some research in the Kremlin library and happened upon a story of Peter the Great, an enormous man with a voracious appetite. According to the document, Peter was served liquor in a huge wooden cup. He downed the lot and exclaimed, "*Vot kak!*"—a Russian term that is used to express surprise. According to Fish, it's possible that this was the origin of the word "vodka." An interesting theory, and a great story, but probably not the original source of the word "vodka."

Who made the first vodka? According to Pokhlebkin, there is no evidence of any type of distilled spirits being made in Russia until the mid-1300s, and it wasn't until the seventeenth century that the term "Moscow vodka" came into common usage. The Poles, on the other hand, in a booklet published by AGROS Foreign Trade Enterprises, claim that *okowita* (another term for "water of life") was being made in their country in the 1400s, and was known as vodka about 100 years earlier than the Russian counterpart. The real question here, however, is: Would we recognize this drink as vodka? And the real answer is a resounding NO.

The medieval vodkas to which both the Russians and the Poles lay claim were distilled spirits, but they were hardly the stuff that we would use to make a vodka Martini. Most of these products were probably flavored with herbs and spices, sometimes to preserve the medicinal qualities of the flavorings and sometimes just to make the drink more palatable. Oddly enough, it is a resurgence of this style of vodka, in the form of all the flavored vodkas currently on the market, that we are seeing today. Some of these products are marvelous creations, many are suitable for chilling and knocking straight back, and others make for marvelous cocktail ingredients, some of which you will see detailed in the Martini recipe chapter of this book.

According to Pokhlebkin, the earliest written occurrence of the word "vodka" in a legal document was in a decree issued in 1751 by Queen Elizabeth I of England, titled *Who Is Permitted to Posses Vats for the Distillation of Vodkas*. The word, however, didn't appear in "any authoritative dictionary of the Russian language, or in reputable literature," until the 1860s. Prior to the invention of the continuous still in the 1830s, a development that made

The distiller fills the tank with wine, or the strained liquid portion of a fermented mash of grains, fruits, sugar, or even vegetables; heats the tank and because alcohol evaporates at a lower temperature than water, the alcohol vapors travel up the neck of the still. There they were collected and then condensed into "low wines," a liquid that

A BELEAGUERED MADISON AVENUE ACCOUNT EXECUTIVE WAS HEARD TO REMARK DURING A PALLIATIVE FIVE P.M. MARTINI THAT HIS MILK ACCOUNT WOULD BE IN MUCH BETTER SHAPE IF HE COULD JUST FIND SOME WAY TO GET PEOPLE FEELING AS SINFUL DRINKING MILK AS THEY DO DRINKING LIQUOR.

GEORGE BISHOP

has a higher proof than the original wine or beer. When the low wines are redistilled, the alcohol content increases again and is further concentrated into "high wines" or liquor. Many whiskies and brandies continue to be made in this type of still because the producers of these spirits seek to make flavorsome products.

It is possible to obtain flavorless high-proof alcohol from a pot still, and indeed, the very popular Ketel One vodka is produced by three distillations in such stills. But Ketel One also employs a technique that was not usually used by distillers until the early 1800s: They discard the first and last portions of newly distilled spirit (known as "foreshots" and "feints" or "heads" and "tails"), and use only the cleaner "center cut" for their vodka. It is improbable that any vodka made prior to the discovery of this technique, and therefore before, say, the 1830s, could have tasted anything like the vodkas we drink today. It's much more likely that the invention of the continuous still gave birth to vodka as we know it, and interestingly enough, this type of still was patented at around the same time that the practice of discarding the heads and tails of spirits made in pot stills became more prevalent.

Sometimes known as the Coffey still and named for its inventor, Aeneas Coffey, the continuous still operates, in very basic terms, by injecting steam into the bottom of a very tall column while a fermented mash is introduced near the top. The steam heats the liquid as it travels down the still, and the alcohol vapors rise to the top of the column and are collected. Some of these stills are gigantic—several stories high—and although lower-proof vapors can be drawn off the still at points below the top, those drawn from the very highest point will be very high in alcohol content—just what is needed when vodka is the goal.

Production

Vodka, as described in the Bureau of Alcohol, Tobacco, and Firearms's (BATF) "Standards of Identity," has three major requirements:

1. Vodka is neutral spirits produced at or above 190 proof and bottled at no less than 80 proof.

It is difficult to distill beverage alcohol at much higher strength than about 96 percent purity (192 proof), and in order to make "pure" alcohol, an expensive technical procedure that bears no relation to distillation must be employed. Vodkas, therefore, run off the still at 190 to 195 proof. Each and every vodka producer, of course, claims to use the best techniques to make its product as pure as possible, and indeed, some of them go to such lengths as to redistill their product as many as four times. The purpose of this effort is to rid their vodka of components known as congeners.

Congeners are impurities, sometimes described as "alcohols with a higher molecular weight than that of ethyl (beverage) alcohol," and these impurities are essential to products such as whiskey, because when whiskey is aged in oak casks, the congeners react with the wood and become, to all intents and purposes, the "flavor" of the whiskey. Vodka, on the other hand, should bear no distinctive flavors, and therefore congeners are looked upon as an unwanted component. Many vodka companies have their products analyzed in order to prove that there are no congeners present, and others will state that it is the congeners in liquor that produce a hangover. While it is possible that some people are allergic to various congeners, hangovers are symptoms of alcohol withdrawal, no matter what type of beverage alcohol—wine, beer, or liquor—has been consumed.

2. Vodka can be made from any material.

Most vodkas are made from grains, some are made from potatoes, and it is possible that some of the very inexpensive bottlings are made from beets, sugar, or any other manner of vegetation. Each distiller will swear that his or her recipe is best, and it is up to each drinker to decide on a personal favorite. As a matter of interest, however, we spoke to one master distiller who used to use a corn-based neutral spirit to make his gin, but when the company switched to a wheat-based spirit, his gin changed character. With a few "tweaks" of the still, however, he soon had his product back to tasting the same as usual. Master distillers are fascinating creatures.

3. Vodka must either be distilled in such a way, or treated after distillation with charcoal and other materials, as to be "without distinctive character, aroma, taste, or color."

And here we enter into the fray. If vodka has no distinctive character, aroma, or taste, why spend a lot of money on a boutique bottling when the least expensive vodka should taste exactly the same as all the rest? Luckily, vodkas do differ from one another, and this was proven to us years ago when we were asked to preside over a vodka tasting. We took eight different bottlings of vodka and poured ourselves servings of each. We looked at each other apprehensively. We nosed, we tasted, we swirled the first vodka around our mouths, and we swallowed minuscule amounts to detect the finish of each product. The differences among the vodkas were nothing short of remarkable. It's true that most of the differential qualities of vodkas lay in the texture or "mouthfeel" of the spirit, but other nuances cropped up with every single bottling.

Simply put, the idiosyncratic techniques that vodka distillers use result in a certain style, and whether that style is nuanced by the type of grains, the water used to cook the grains, the type of still, the number of distillations, or the materials through which the distillate is filtered, the fact remains that vodkas differ. And as you will see in the notes alongside the various bottlings of vodka, the techniques employed to make each product can vary significantly.

Brands and Bottlings

Absolut Vodka
Made in Sweden, 40% alcohol by volume

Sweden has a long and rich history of vodka production, and Absolut vodka plays an interesting role in it. When he was just a young man, Lars Olsen Smith, a Swede who would come to be known as the King of Vodka, started work in the Swedish spirits industry. Astonishingly, by the early 1870s, he controlled more than half of Sweden's vodka business. But Smith faced a problem with the bureaucracy in Stockholm, since the city not only produced its own vodka, but also had a monopoly on sales within its geographical limits.

Smith, a staunch advocate of free trade, was upset. His brand-new distillery was equipped with continuous stills, and since his vodka was the purest being made in Sweden at the time, he named his product *Absolut renat Brannvin* (absolutely pure vodka). His vodka was very popular, but the people of Stockholm couldn't buy it within the city limits. Mr. Smith donned his thinking cap and made haste in opening a retail outlet on Reimer's

Island, just outside the jurisdiction of Stockholm. But he didn't stop there; in order to encourage city dwellers to buy his vodka, he offered free boat rides to the island. To the dismay of the local government, Stockholmers streamed to the ferry and traveled to Reimer's Island to buy Smith's vodka. The result: Absolut success.

In 1906, Smith's son, Otto, followed in his father's footsteps by becoming a cofounder of the distillery that now produces Absolut vodka, and ironically, the distillery is now owned by the Absolut Company, a division of V&S Vin & Sprit AB—the state-owned Swedish spirits and wine company.

Production

Absolut vodka is made in Åhus, a small town on Sweden's Baltic coast. Well water is used to make the vodka from a mash of 100 percent wheat, and the vodka is distilled a total of four times in continuous stills before it is deemed Absolut-ly pure. The spirit is then brought down to proof with the same well water before it is bottled. Absolut vodka is not filtered prior to bottling: "Charcoal is for barbecues," says Lars Nellmer, Marketing Director for the Absolut Company. "We rely on our distinctive distillation methods to produce a pure product that still bears character."

Tasting Notes

Faint lemon/pine aroma;
clean and crisp palate with a slight taste
of baked bread; very light finish.
Highly recommended.

Belvedere Vodka

Made in Poland, 40% alcohol by volume

Belvedere Polish vodka has been available in Europe since the early 1990s and was introduced to the United States in 1996.

Production

Belvedere is made from 100 percent rye grain. The mash is first distilled in a pot still and then undergoes three more distillations in continuous stills before being filtered three times through two different types of carbon.

Tasting Notes

Hints of grain, slightly astringent;
thick syrupy-peppery palate; smooth, warm finish.
Recommended.

Boord's Vodka

Made in the U.S., 40% alcohol by volume

Boord & Son was a company established in England in 1726, but in the United States, the label now belongs to the David Sherman Corporation of St. Louis, Missouri. Originally, Boord's was known as a gin distillery, and they produced one of the original "Old Tom" gins (see page 53). Boord's Vodka is a 100 percent grain-based spirit.

Tasting Notes

Flat nose with perfume/alcohol notes;
clean, clear palate; fast finish—totally gone.

Burnett's Premium Classic Vodka

Made in the U.S., 40% alcohol by volume

See Sir Robert Burnett's Distilled London Dry Gin, page 74.

Production

Burnett's is a grain-based vodka distilled out at about 96 percent pure alcohol and triple filtered through charcoal.

The distiller fills the tank with wine, or the strained liquid portion of a fermented mash of grains, fruits, sugar, or even vegetables; heats the tank and because alcohol evaporates at a lower temperature than water, the alcohol vapors travel up the neck of the still. There they were collected and then condensed into "low wines," a liquid that has a higher proof than the original wine or beer. When the low wines are redistilled, the alcohol content increases again and is further concentrated into "high wines" or liquor. Many whiskies and brandies continue to be made in this type of still because the producers of these spirits seek to make flavorsome products.

It is possible to obtain flavorless high-proof alcohol from a pot still, and indeed, the very popular Ketel One vodka is produced by three distillations in such stills. But Ketel One also employs a technique that was not usually used by distillers until the early 1800s: They discard the first and last portions of newly distilled spirit (known as "foreshots" and "feints" or "heads" and "tails"), and use only the cleaner "center cut" for their vodka. It is improb-

> A BELEAGUERED MADISON AVENUE ACCOUNT EXECUTIVE WAS HEARD TO REMARK DURING A PALLIATIVE FIVE P.M. MARTINI THAT HIS MILK ACCOUNT WOULD BE IN MUCH BETTER SHAPE IF HE COULD JUST FIND SOME WAY TO GET PEOPLE FEELING AS SINFUL DRINKING MILK AS THEY DO DRINKING LIQUOR.
>
> GEORGE BISHOP

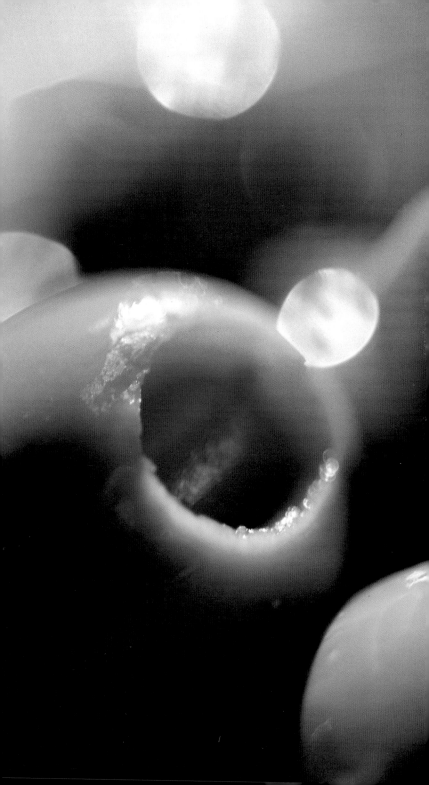

it is the congeners in liquor that produce a hangover. While it is possible that some people are allergic to various congeners, hangovers are symptoms of alcohol withdrawal, no matter what type of beverage alcohol—wine, beer, or liquor—has been consumed.

2. Vodka can be made from any material.

Most vodkas are made from grains, some are made from potatoes, and it is possible that some of the very inexpensive bottlings are made from beets, sugar, or any other manner of vegetation. Each distiller will swear that his or her recipe is best, and it is up to each drinker to decide on a personal favorite. As a matter of interest, however, we spoke to one master distiller who used to use a corn-based neutral spirit to make his gin, but when the company switched to a wheat-based spirit, his gin changed character. With a few "tweaks" of the still, however, he soon had his product back to tasting the same as usual. Master distillers are fascinating creatures.

3. Vodka must either be distilled in such a way, or treated after distillation with charcoal and other materials, as to be "without distinctive character, aroma, taste, or color."

And here we enter into the fray. If vodka has no distinctive character, aroma, or taste, why spend a lot of money on a boutique bottling when the least expensive vodka should taste exactly the same as all the rest? Luckily, vodkas do differ from one another, and this was proven to us years ago when we were asked to preside over a vodka tasting. We took eight different bottlings of vodka and poured ourselves servings of each. We looked at each other apprehensively. We nosed, we tasted, we swirled the first vodka around our mouths, and we swallowed minuscule amounts to detect the finish of each product. The differences among the vodkas were nothing short of remarkable. It's true that most of the differential qualities of vodkas lay in the texture or "mouthfeel" of the spirit, but other nuances cropped up with every single bottling.

Simply put, the idiosyncratic techniques that vodka distillers use result in a certain style, and whether that style is nuanced by the type of grains, the water used to cook the grains, the type of still, the number of distillations, or the materials through which the distillate is filtered, the fact remains that vodkas differ. And as you will see in the notes alongside the various bottlings of vodka, the techniques employed to make each product can vary significantly.

Brands and Bottlings

Absolut Vodka
Made in Sweden, 40% alcohol by volume

Sweden has a long and rich history of vodka production, and Absolut vodka plays an interesting role in it. When he was just a young man, Lars Olsen Smith, a Swede who would come to be known as the King of Vodka, started work in the Swedish spirits industry. Astonishingly, by the early 1870s, he controlled more than half of Sweden's vodka business. But Smith faced a problem with the bureaucracy in Stockholm, since the city not only produced its own vodka, but also had a monopoly on sales within its geographical limits.

Smith, a staunch advocate of free trade, was upset. His brand-new distillery was equipped with continuous stills, and since his vodka was the purest being made in Sweden at the time, he named his product *Absolut renat Brannvin* (absolutely pure vodka). His vodka was very popular, but the people of Stockholm couldn't buy it within the city limits. Mr. Smith donned his thinking cap and made haste in opening a retail outlet on Reimer's

Island, just outside the jurisdiction of Stockholm. But he didn't stop there; in order to encourage city dwellers to buy his vodka, he offered free boat rides to the island. To the dismay of the local government, Stockholmers streamed to the ferry and traveled to Reimer's Island to buy Smith's vodka. The result: Absolut success.

In 1906, Smith's son, Otto, followed in his father's footsteps by becoming a cofounder of the distillery that now produces Absolut vodka, and ironically, the distillery is now owned by the Absolut Company, a division of V&S Vin & Sprit AB—the state-owned Swedish spirits and wine company.

Production

Absolut vodka is made in Åhus, a small town on Sweden's Baltic coast. Well water is used to make the vodka from a mash of 100 percent wheat, and the vodka is distilled a total of four times in continuous stills before it is deemed Absolut-ly pure. The spirit is then brought down to proof with the same well water before it is bottled. Absolut vodka is not filtered prior to bottling: "Charcoal is for barbecues," says Lars Nellmer, Marketing Director for the Absolut Company. "We rely on our distinctive distillation methods to produce a pure product that still bears character."

Tasting Notes

Faint lemon/pine aroma;
clean and crisp palate with a slight taste
of baked bread; very light finish.
Highly recommended.

Belvedere Vodka

Made in Poland, 40% alcohol by volume

Belvedere Polish vodka has been available in Europe since the early 1990s and was introduced to the United States in 1996.

Production

Belvedere is made from 100 percent rye grain. The mash is first distilled in a pot still and then undergoes three more distillations in continuous stills before being filtered three times through two different types of carbon.

Tasting Notes

Hints of grain, slightly astringent;
thick syrupy-peppery palate; smooth, warm finish.
Recommended.

Boord's Vodka
Made in the U.S., 40% alcohol by volume

Boord & Son was a company established in England in 1726, but in the United States, the label now belongs to the David Sherman Corporation of St. Louis, Missouri. Originally, Boord's was known as a gin distillery, and they produced one of the original "Old Tom" gins (see page 53). Boord's Vodka is a 100 percent grain-based spirit.

Tasting Notes

Flat nose with perfume/alcohol notes;
clean, clear palate; fast finish—totally gone.

Burnett's Premium Classic Vodka
Made in the U.S., 40% alcohol by volume

See Sir Robert Burnett's Distilled London Dry Gin, page 74.

Production

Burnett's is a grain-based vodka distilled out at about 96 percent pure alcohol and triple filtered through charcoal.

Tasting Notes

*Silky, fresh nose; supple, medium body that's
pleasantly simple; clean, quick finish.*

Cardinal Ultimate Vodka
Made in Holland, 45% alcohol by volume

Cardinal Ultimate is made by the Uto distillery, a business that has been in existence in Holland since 1777, and although Uto started life as a producer of genever-style gin, the company has been making vodka since the early years of the twentieth century. The Uto distillery claims that, at that time, the cardinal was used as a symbol for vodka when it was shipped to foreign countries that may not have understood the word "vodka."

Production

Cardinal Ultimate vodka is made from a very secret process and is said to incorporate botanicals that produce character rather than flavor—hence the spirit is flavorless and can be labeled as vodka. This is a combination of spirits made from grains and sugar beets that are distilled three times in pot stills, carefully filtered, and brought down to proof before bottling.

Tasting Notes

Peppery, fresh nose;

thick, smooth, elegant body that's flavorless

but full of character; clean, crisp, short finish.

Highly recommended.

Denaka Vodka

Made in Denmark, 40% alcohol by volume

Denaka vodka was originally produced in the early 1980s, when Scandinavian vodkas were becoming so popular in the United States. The idea for the product came from a Frenchman who commissioned the vodka to be made by Danisco Distillers in Dalby, Denmark, some forty miles south of Copenhagen. After changing ownership a few times, Denaka was finally made available nationwide in the United States in 1989.

Production

Denaka is made from 100 percent wheat and demineralized water that flows from what the company describes as an "orchard water supply." It is filtered through activated carbon before being brought down to proof and bottled.

> I MUST GET OUT OF THESE WET CLOTHES
> AND INTO A DRY MARTINI.
> ATTRIBUTED TO ROBERT CHARLES BENCHLEY

Gordon's Vodka
Made in the U.S., 40% alcohol by volume

See Gordon's Distilled London Dry Gin, page 82.

Production

Gordon's is made from a 100 percent grain mash, and the company pledges that no additives find their way into its vodka.

Tasting Notes

Bland but inviting nose; very clean palate with hints of toffee; smooth, warm finish. Recommended.

Hertekamp Vodka
Made in Belgium, 40% alcohol by volume

Hertekamp is made in Belgium by Distillers Bruggeman, a company started by Pieter Bruggeman in 1884 to produce grain-based liqueurs and genever-style gins.

Production

Distillers Bruggeman boasts that this vodka is the result of traditional craftsmanship and high technology, and claims that theirs was the first environmentally friendly distillery in Belgium.

Tasting Notes

Clean, spicy nose, lots of character; very pleasant thick, luscious, clean body; thick, warm, soothing finish.
Highly recommended.

Ketel One Imported Dutch Vodka
Made in Holland, 40% alcohol by volume

The Nolet family, producers of this vodka, were originally grain traders who opened a distillery in 1691 to make genever gin and liqueurs. The company supplied the royal Romanov family with spirits, and in 1804 were granted the right to exhibit the double eagle from the Czar's crest on their products. "Ketel One" refers to a 180-year-old pot still that still is used today to produce its eponymous vodka. Luckily, that still was hidden underground during World War II when Axis forces confiscated all of the copper that could be found.

Production

Ketel One is a 100 percent wheat-based, triple-distilled vodka that undergoes its final distillation in the coal-fired "Ketel One" copper pot still. The water used to make this spirit comes from nearby sand dunes and is filtered through sand and then cleaned before being used. After distillation, Ketel One is rested in tiled tanks for a period of six weeks. It is then tasted by a member of the Nolet family and, if it is deemed suitable, is bottled.

Tasting Notes

Wonderful cereal aroma; a full, round body that coats the whole mouth; notes of fresh-baked bread; remarkably smooth finish. Highly recommended.

Luksusowa Polish Luxury Potato Vodka

Made in Poland, 40% alcohol by volume

Poland has a rich history of vodka production and is the major contender, with Russia, in the "who was first to make vodka" debate. The word Luksusowa (LUX-us-OH-ver) is Polish for "luxury" or "luxurious," and at the 1988 World Selection of Wines, Liquors, Spirits, and

Liqueurs, in Athens, this vodka was awarded the competition's highest honor, the *"Medal avec Palmes."*

Production

Luksusowa is made from 100 percent potatoes grown in the light soil alongside the Baltic Sea. The mineral-free water used in the production process comes from artesian wells, and this same water is used to reduce the final distillate to bottling proof. Luksusowa is triple-distilled and filtered through charcoal and oak chips.

Tasting Notes

*A mossy aroma; medium body; a sweet,
almost candy-like palate with a thick, syrupy finish.
Recommended.*

Moskovskaya Genuine Russian Vodka
Made in Russia, 40% alcohol by volume

Moskovskaya, named for Moscow, is marketed in the United States by the same company that brings us Stolichnaya. This is a grain-based vodka made with soft glacial water and filtered through activated charcoal. Moskovskaya is the top-selling Russian vodka in Canada.

Tasting Notes

Grainy nose with hints of citrus;
plain and spicy in mouth; clean, quick finish.

———— ((●)) ————

Perlova Premium Vodka
Made in the Ukraine, 40% alcohol by volume

Perlova is a 100 percent wheat vodka made with soft spring water from the Carpathian Mountains of the Ukraine and filtered twice, once through quartz crystal, then through birch charcoal. The company marketing this product claims that the same recipe has been used to make this vodka for more than 400 years.

Tasting Notes

Clover/grainy nose; thick bodied with caramel notes;
long, smooth finish with distinct coffee notes.

———— ((●)) ————

Priviet Vodka
Made in Russia, 40% alcohol by volume

Priviet, meaning something akin to "best regards," was introduced in the United States in 1989. This vodka is sold in Russia under the brand name Pshenichnaya. It is made from select winter wheat and glacial water.

Tasting Notes

Rich nose; slightly salty on palate—would do well in a Bloody Mary; spicy, short finish.

"Tax Time for the Nation—Martini Time for Washington"

OZIO, A WASHINGTON, D.C. RESTAURANT, OFFERED A LITTLE RELIEF FOR TAXPAYERS IN 1996. ON APRIL 15TH THE RESTAURANT REPORTEDLY OFFERED A FREE MARTINI TO EVERYONE WHO BROUGHT A TAX RETURN TO THE RESTAURANT, AND TO EVERY CPA WHO PRODUCED A BUSINESS CARD.

Rain Vodka

Made in the U.S., 40% alcohol by volume

Rain, introduced in 1996, is the first vodka to be made from organically grown American grain. To accentuate the environmentally concerned attitude of this product, both the labels on the bottle and the cartons used for shipping are made from recycled paper—but that's not all. The Sazerac Company of New Orleans, producers of Rain, has not only made "a sizable contribution" to the Wilderness Society, it has also pledged to make additional contributions for each bottle of Rain sold. The label notes the year the grains used for that bottle were harvested.

P r o d u c t i o n

The grain used to make Rain is grown at the certified-organic Fizzle Flat Farms in Yale, Illinois. The mash is made from Kentucky water, which filters naturally through limestone, and then is distilled four times. Two filterings—one through diamond dust and another through activated charcoal—occur before bottling.

T a s t i n g   N o t e s

Hints of caramel on nose and palate;
flat and bland yet characterful palate, slightly syrupy;
short finish. Recommended.

Rainbow Vodka

Made in the U.S., 40% alcohol by volume

Rainbow vodka is a new spirit produced by Marie Brizard Wines & Spirits, U.S.A., a company that also makes Rainbow gin, rum, tequila, and triple sec. The company pledges that "fifty percent of the net profits from the sales of Rainbow spirits will be donated to local non-profit organizations that conduct research and/or clinical drug testing for HIV/AIDS patients in the hopes to find a cure for this non-discriminating disease."

Tasting Notes

Clear, smooth alcohol nose;
slightly spicy and fresh on palate, fairly astringent;
long, slightly sour finish.

Skyy Vodka
Made in the U.S., 40% alcohol by volume

When Skyy Vodka was first made available in the United States, it caused quite a stir. According to a 1994 article in the *San Francisco Examiner,* the owner of Skyy, Maurice Kanbar, attributed the success of his vodka, partially, to a study that revealed that people who drank liquors that were very pure were overwhelmingly headache-free in the morning. Kanbar was referring to the lack of congeners in his vodka.

Various people took Kanbar to task about this theory, but whereas hangovers are usually thought to be merely the effects of alcohol withdrawal, it is possible that some people are also allergic to various congeners, and therefore, Kanbar's very pure vodka would, indeed, be beneficial to such folk. As a matter of interest, Kanbar is an inventor with over thirty patents to his name, one of which is the "D-Fuzz-It," a device for removing pills from woolen clothing.

Catch Up Now

HUMPHREY BOGART IS CREDITED WITH COMPLAINING THAT THE TROUBLE WITH THE WORLD IS THAT EVERYBODY IN IT IS THREE DRINKS BEHIND.

Production

Skyy is an American grain-based vodka that is distilled four times, each distillation at a different temperature in order to remove specific congeners. The spirit then goes through a patent-pending three-step filtration system to remove any remaining impurities before the vodka is bottled.

Tasting Notes

A clean, crisp aroma with an ever-so-slightly nutty palate; the vodka disappears in the throat. Highly recommended.

Smirnoff Vodka
Made in the U.S., 40% alcohol by volume

Smirnoff Black Traditional Russian Vodka
Made in Russia, 40% alcohol by volume

The Pierre A. Smirnoff Company opened in Moscow in 1864 and was appointed purveyor to the Court of His Imperial Majesty, Czar Alexander III, in 1886. According to Heublein, Inc., the company that owns the Smirnoff label, in 1933, a Russian by the name of Rudolf Kunett bought the formula for Smirnoff vodka from Vladimir Smirnoff, an émigré to France during the Russian Revolution of 1917. It was, more or less, common knowledge that Prohibition in the United States would be repealed in 1933 (it didn't actually happen until December of that year), and Kunett planned to open America's first vodka distillery, using the Smirnoff name and formula.

The distillery was far from successful, and in 1939, John G. Martin, an executive from the company then known as G. F. Heublein & Brothers, bought Smirnoff for a reputed $14,000 plus royalties. But vodka still wasn't very popular. Then came Jack Morgan. Owner of the Cock n' Bull restaurant in Hollywood, Morgan had a sizable inventory of ginger beer on hand. This delightful soda is spicy, with much heavier ginger flavors and a far drier palate than ginger ale. But like vodka, Americans just weren't buying it. Martin and Morgan put their heads, and their products, together and created the Moscow Mule—a mixture of vodka and ginger beer, classically served in a copper mug and garnished with a wedge of lime. It's a wonderful drink—but how would these guys make it popular?

The earliest Polaroid camera was marketed in 1948, and John G. Martin armed himself with this new invention when he toured the finest bars in New York City to persuade bartenders that the Moscow Mule was a drink they should offer to their customers. He also took along a copper mug and a bottle of vodka. The bartenders, of course, were champing at the bit to have their photographs taken with this incredible new invention, and they dutifully posed for photographs that Martin used to promote his vodka. Thus, in the latter years of the 1940s, vodka began to gain in popularity in the United States.

Production

The "Red Label" Smirnoff is a grain-based vodka made in the United States and filtered through "a mountain charcoal, through quartz again, and after being rested in stainless-steel holding tanks, finally through cloth. Stolichnaya Gold is also made with glacial water and winter wheat, but it is distilled four times before it is brought down to bottle proof with the same water used in the mashing process.

Tasting Notes

Stolichnaya Genuine Russian Vodka

A rich, slightly oily body with a somewhat perfumey palate. The texture is silky and peppers the tongue, and the finish is delightfully smooth. Recommended.

TO BEGIN WITH, YOU TAKE TWO OUNCES OF STOLICHNAYA—
80 OR 100 PROOF, DEPENDING ENTIRELY ON THE WEIGHT
OF YOUR PELOTAS—WHICH YOU POUR OVER ICE. YOU THEN
DROP IN A GREEK BLACK OLIVE FOR THE BITTER OF LIFE,
AND RIM THE GLASS WITH ORANGE RIND FOR THE SWEET OF
LIFE. YOU THEN FLAME THE DRINK FOR THE FIRE OF LIFE
AND, ALTHOUGH THE FLAME LASTS FOR BUT A SECOND, IN
YOUR BODY THE FIRE WILL BURN FOR HOURS. WITH OR
WITHOUT THE MATCH, YOU STILL WIND UP WITH THE
WORLD'S GREATEST MARTINI.

JOSEPH WAMBAUGH
TO *PLAYBOY*, DESCRIBING A MARTINI
HE MADE WITH PETER MONAHAN

Vodka

Stolichnaya Gold
Ultra Premium Vodka

*A huge, full body and a palate that's full
of character. It offers a tingling, peppery mouthful
and a thick, almost syrupy finish. Highly recommended.*

Taaka Platinum Vodka

Made in the U.S., 40% alcohol by volume

Production

Taaka Platinum vodka is triple distilled and filtered through charcoal.

Tasting Notes

*White winy/floral nose; medium body with grain notes
and some spice; clean finish. Recommended.*

Tanqueray Sterling Vodka

Made in England, 40% alcohol by volume

The Tanqueray company found a document hidden deep
in their archives that indicates that Charles Tanqueray

(see Tanqueray gin, page 88) made and sold neutral spirits (basically vodka), as well as gin, in the 1800s. His still, nicknamed "Old Tom," is used today to make Tanqueray Sterling vodka.

Production

Tanqueray Sterling is a grain-based vodka made with water from Scotland and distilled twice before being filtered through red ochil granite chips.

Tasting Notes

Soothing clean, clear nose;
very pleasant medium body with slight hints of citrus;
long, warm finish. Highly recommended.

Teton Glacier Hand-Crafted American Potato Vodka
Made in the U.S., 40% alcohol by volume

A brand-new product in 1996, here's an American vodka that's produced at the Silver Creek Distillery in Rigby, Ohio, solely from select Idaho potatoes and pure well water from the Rocky Mountains. The spirit goes through a four-column, triple-distilling process and is filtered through both charcoal and garnet crystal before being bottled. Details of the filtration system, which was developed by Teton's chief distiller Adam Ackerman, are proprietary, but we have been told that this is one of the most complex systems in the world.

Tasting Notes

Crystal-clear nose; big body, very clean
with lots of character. Highly recommended.

ACCORDING TO AN ARTICLE THAT APPEARED IN THE MARCH 9, 1962 ISSUE OF *TIME* MAGAZINE, TENNESSEE WILLIAMS CHASED AWAY "THE FIRST TENSION SPOOK OF THE DAY WITH AN ICE-COLD MARTINI." THIS APPARENTLY HAPPENED TO WILLIAMS AFTER WRITING FOR ABOUT AN HOUR AND A HALF.

Tvarscki Vodka
Made in the U.S., 40% alcohol by volume

An American vodka with a Russian-sounding name, Tvarscki is a grain-based vodka.

Tasting Notes

Fresh/alcohol nose; very dry/astringent on palate;
short finish with slight powdery aftertaste.

Ultraa, The Ultimate Modern World Russian Vodka

Made in Russia, 40% alcohol by volume

Production

Ultraa is a 100 percent grain vodka brought down to bottling proof with water from Russia's Lake Lagodas. The water is said to be filtered through "natural quartz sands and semi-precious stones," and "oxygen-saturated to provide . . . crystal clarity." The spirit is then filtered through eight meters of activated birch charcoal.

Tasting Notes

Fresh, cold nose; medium body with nice spiciness; crisp, spicy finish. Recommended.

ONE WAY TO FIND OUT WHAT KIND OF PLACE YOU ARE ABOUT TO DINE IN IS TO ORDER, SAY, A VERY DRY MARTINI AT THE BAR, WATCH IT BEING MADE, DRINK IT AND THEN GO TO YOUR TABLE. ORDER A SECOND VERY DRY MARTINI AND, IF IT TASTES LIKE A DIFFERENT DRINK, PAY YOUR CHECK AND LEAVE BECAUSE THE CHANCES ARE THAT THE FOOD WON'T BE ANY BETTER.

GEORGE BISHOP

Virgin Vodka

Made in the United Kingdom,
40% alcohol by volume

Available in the United States only since 1996, Virgin vodka is very popular in Great Britain. Virgin vodka is made from 100 percent grain, and after being distilled once, the spirit is diluted, and distilled two more times. The dilution process, called "purification" by the company, is said to improve the taste and aroma of the vodka. After the third distillation, Virgin vodka is put through "further extractions," and "carefully controlled levels of filtration" before being bottled.

Tasting Notes

Slightly sweetish nose, very bland on palate;
medium finish; nicely bland.

Volganaya Vodka

Made in Estonia, 40% alcohol by volume

Volganaya is produced at the Liviko distillery, a state-owned plant in Tallinn, Estonia (described by the company as "Old Russia"). The city claims to have a

500-year distilling tradition, and this particular distillery has been making Volganaya ("the best vodka they produce") for sixty years. It was first imported to the United States in 1992 by Jeff Cohen, a business professor at Santa Clara University, and Brian Robinson, an oral surgeon.

Tasting Notes

Spicy nose with hints of perfume;
thick body with same perfume on palate; perfume lingers.

Wolfschmidt Vodka
Made in the U.S., 40% alcohol by volume

The Wolfschmidt name, in connection to vodka, dates to 1847, when the Wolfschmidt family began distilling vodka in Russia. The Wolfschmidts are said to have been purveyors of vodka to Russian Czars Alexander III and Nicholas II. This is a grain-based vodka that is made in the United States.

Tasting Notes

Clean nose; big body with pleasant sweetness;
smooth finish.

Wyborowa Vodka

Made in Poland, 40% alcohol by volume

Production

Wyborowa (VEE-ber-OH-ver), a grain-based Polish vodka, is touted as "premium 3x3 vodka," meaning that the grains are triple cleaned, the alcohol is triple distilled, and the vodka is triple filtered.

Tasting Notes

Cold, slightly sweet nose;
thick and spicy yet neutral on palate;
clean, hot finish.

Vermouth

———◇/◇/◇———

THE WORD "VERMOUTH" IS PROBABLY DERIVED from either the German *wermut* or *vermut* or possibly the Old English *wermod*, all meaning wormwood. In *The Book of Drinking*, author John Doxat states that it was an Italian gentleman returning from Bavaria who introduced *vermutwein* (wormwood wine) to Paris in the late 1500s. But wine flavored with wormwood has been said to date back to Hippocrates himself. Wormwood, a bitter herb, has been used for centuries as a treatment for parasites, and because Hippocrates is known to have infused wines with various herbs for medicinal purposes, it is quite likely that he did indeed make an early form of vermouth.

There are vague references to wines that could have been vermouth in the Piedmont region of Italy in the late 1600s, but it is commonly thought that during that period, vermouth was actually a concentration of herbs in wine and was consumed only when diluted with ordinary wine. It wasn't until 1786, when Antonio Benedetto

Carpano produced the first commercial branded bottling of vermouth, that this style of apéritif wine officially was born. Carpano still produces vermouths, but all of them are of the sweet, or Italian style, and the most famous bottling produced by them is Punt e Mes, a delightful mixture of sweet vermouth and bitters.

In 1800, however, a certain Joseph Noilly created a new style of vermouth in Marseillan, and dry, or French, vermouth—the style used to make a Dry Martini—had finally arrived. In 1813, Noilly teamed up with Claudius Prat, and together produced and marketed Noilly Prat vermouth. Other companies would soon follow suit, and even the Italians were not too far behind in producing a dry, French style of vermouth.

Vermouth was being exported to the United States by many of the older major producers by the mid-1800s, but initially, it was sweet vermouth that was the more popular style in this country. Indeed, all of the cocktail recipe books we have seen that were published prior to 1895 called merely for "vermouth," and that vermouth was definitely sweet. We still hark back to the initial producers of sweet and dry vermouths, however, when we describe vermouth as Italian or French, although both styles are produced, not only in Italy and France, but in many other wine-producing countries around the world.

How Vermouth Is Made

Vermouth is a fortified, aromatized wine, that is, a wine that has been fortified by spirits, usually brandy, and aromatized by a variety of botanicals. The governmental "standards of identity" for vermouth define the product as being an apéritif wine having an alcoholic content of not less than 15 percent (30 proof) that has had brandy or alcohol flavored with herbs added to it, and bears "the taste, aroma, and characteristics generally attributed to vermouth."

As is the case with gin, the precise recipe for each vermouth is a well-guarded secret to each individual producer; however, common herbs and spices used include calamus root, camomile, centaury, clove, coriander, elderflowers, gentian, hyssop, mace, marjoram, nutmeg, orange peel, oregano, orris root, quinine, sage, sandalwood, and, of course, wormwood.

Production

Some of the techniques used by vermouth producers are proprietary secrets. It is rumored that some producers merely add oils, essences, or other flavorings to fortified wine to make their vermouths, but the more reputable companies actually go to great lengths to make their products from scratch. The following production notes, therefore, are merely an indication of how good vermouths are made.

It would be somewhat erroneous to say that vermouths are made from inferior wines—indeed, some producers are very proud of the carefully selected wines on which they base their vermouths—but it does make sense that wines without a great deal of character would be used to make a style of wine that is favored more for the qualities of its additional ingredients than those of the primary wine.

Many of the top-quality vermouths are made from aged wine, and all vermouths—sweet and dry—are made from white wines. The wine is then fortified and sweetened by the addition of *mistelle,* a mixture of unfermented grape juice and brandy, and sometimes sugar is added at this point. The fortified wine is then flavored with botanicals; some companies prefer to let the wine soak up the flavors of the various herbs and spices for a period of weeks, and others choose to gently heat the wine, thus speeding up the process. Accordingly, some producers distill fruit-based liquors and add those to their vermouths, while still others steep their botanicals in brandy before using it to fortify their wines. To further complicate matters—and

Tasting Notes

*Colorless with complex nose—hints of almonds
and/or oranges and mint; round, luscious, complex
palate with sharp, dry fruitiness and herbal notes;
long, dry, crisp finish. Highly recommended.*

Cinzano Extra Dry Vermouth
Made in Italy, 18% alcohol by volume

In 1757, Carlo Stefano Cinzano, a distiller's son, began
selling a sweet aromatized wine in the village of Pecetto,
close to Turin, an area that was already the center of the
Italian vermouth industry. Cinzano's descendants moved
the company to Turin in 1816, and by the 1850s, Cinzano vermouth was being exported to the United States.

Production

Cinzano Extra Dry Vermouth is made from a Trebbiano
wine that is fortified with neutral grape spirits and then
blended with up to fifty varieties of herbs, spices, barks,
and/or fruit peels. The flavorings—mainly wormwood,
coriander, elder, cloves, marjoram, and summer savory—
are produced by maceration, distillation, and/or infusion
of the botanicals.

Tasting Notes

Colorless with appealing sweet, herbal/floral nose;
light bodied and winy in mouth; warm, dry, herbal finish
and aftertaste. Recommended.

Dubonnet Blanc

Made in the U.S., 19% alcohol by volume

Dubonnet, an "apéritif wine" created in 1846 by French wine merchant Joseph Dubonnet, is not a true vermouth, and we have rarely heard of it being used in Dry Martinis. However, because we were tasting Lillet (another "apéritif wine"), we thought the Dubonnet deserved equal consideration. We were both surprised and delighted by the result.

Tasting Notes

Pale straw color with rich, oaky, complex nose;
very balanced palate with play of lemon
and herbs plus rich, honey/caramel notes;
excellent, long finish—herby, fruity, and dry—
that runs the gamut of all that came before.
Highly recommended.

Lillet Blanc Apéritif Wine
Made in France, 18% alcohol by volume

Like Dubbonet Blanc, Lillet is classified as an apéritif wine, not a vermouth. But since so many Martini lovers use this delightful product, we just couldn't omit it here. Raymond and Paul Lillet created their eponymous product in 1872 in Podensac, a village on the Garonne River, just south of Bordeaux, and originally it was known as Kina-Lillet, *Kina* being the French abbreviation for quinine. The fame of Lillet soon spread to Africa, Argentina, Mexico, and Britain, and it was first exported to the United States in 1910. At one point, most of the company was in the hands of the American firm, Schenley, but it was purchased by a consortium of French vintners, headed by Bruno-Eugène Borie, in 1985.

Production

The wines used in Lillet Blanc vary according to quality and availability and are made from Muscadelle, Sémillon, and Sauvignon blanc grapes, which are married to ten secret "fruit liqueurs." These so-called liqueurs are actually French brandies that have been cold-macerated with the fruits for four to six months. The ratio of wine to brandies is 85:15, and although the recipe is secret, the company does mention including both sweet and bitter oranges from Spain and Morocco and quinine from Ecuador in the process. After the wines and fruit-infused brandies are mingled together, Lillet spends a full year aging in oak casks before it is bottled.

The company produces 50,000 cases of Lillet (Blanc and Rouge) annually, and it recommends that the products be recorked and refrigerated after opening.

Tasting Notes

Pale straw color with winy, lilac nose;
medium-bodied with lots of citrus—lemon, grapefruit,
and orange—plus appealing herbal notes;
warm, pleasant, medium finish. Recommended.

Martini & Rossi Extra Dry Vermouth
Made in Italy, 18% alcohol by volume

The company that was to become Martini & Rossi was established when Alessandro Martini, Teofilo Sola, and Luigi Rossi took over a Turin-based vermouth company in 1863. The enterprising trio started to export their vermouth to the United States that same year. In time, the company moved to Pessione, closer to the port city of Genoa, in order to make exportation of their products easier. The ploy worked, and some five years later their vermouths were being shipped to Brazil, Argentina, Greece, Portugal, Belgium, Switzerland, Egypt, and Turkey. Sola's shares in the firm were bought by Rossi in 1879, and the company then became Martini & Rossi.

Production

Martini & Rossi not only goes to great lengths to make its vermouths and, surprisingly, is also fairly free with information on how it is done. The exception, of course, the precise recipe for its botanicals. The list of herbs "available," and supplied to us by the company, however, includes some we haven't seen in other recipes—lungwort, lungmoss, rhubarb, and speedwell, among them. These are, of course, in addition to the wormwood and other herbs and spices found in most vermouth recipes.

The recipe involves a two-step process: The herbal botanicals are added to an unspecified type of diluted alcohol and distilled; the spices are macerated, thus without heating them, in alcohol. The results of both steps are blended with light-bodied base wines and then the mixture is aged for three to six months. Finally, the vermouth is cold-stabilized and filtered before bottling.

Tasting Notes

Colorless with sweet, sugar candy nose;
medium-bodied with dry palate and faint herbal notes;
long, dry finish with herbs and fruits.
Recommended.

Noilly Prat Original
French Dry Vermouth
Made in France, 18% alcohol by volume

Noilly Prat (NOY-ee-ee praht) vermouth was originally produced in France in 1813, when Joseph Noilly of Lyon teamed up with Claudius Prat to produce a style of vermouth that Noilly had created some thirteen years previously. This was the first example of dry vermouth, as opposed to the sweet variety that had originated in Italy, and it is probably the reason that today so many people refer to dry vermouth as "French" and sweet vermouth as "Italian"—no matter where they were produced. Noilly Prat was first marketed in the United States in 1853.

Production

As far as we know, no other company goes to as much trouble in aging its vermouth as does Noilly Prat. The two white wines used in the production of this vermouth are Picpoul and Clairette. Initially, the wines are aged separately, for almost a year, in huge vats made from Canadian oak, a wood chosen because of its low tannin content. After this initial aging, the wines are transferred to smaller casks that are left in the open air for a further twelve months, during which time six to eight percent of their volume evaporates. After this stage the wines are transferred to large vats and are moved to cool cellars to rest for several months.

When well-rested, the two wines are mingled together and sweetened and softened by the addition of a small amount of *mistelle* (incompletely fermented grape must) and fruit eaux-de-vie. This mixture is returned to the smaller vats, and the botanicals are added. Every day for a period of three weeks, the vats are stirred, and finally the wine is strained from the botanicals and rested for a further six weeks. After all that work, the vermouth is finally ready to be cold-stabilized and prepared for bottling.

Of course, the exact ingredients used are a company secret, but Noilly Prat claims that its eaux-de-vie are made from fresh fruits that are distilled separately, and that its dry vermouth contains the natural flavors of twenty herbs, while its sweet vermouth bottling calls for thirty herbs. The company recommends that once opened, bottles should be resealed and refrigerated, where they will keep for up to six months.

Tasting Notes

Colorless with rich, slightly lemony nose; silky body with herbal notes and tons of character; long, fresh, dry finish with clean, refreshing aftertaste. Highly recommended.

Stock Imported Extra Dry White Vermouth
Made in Italy, 18% alcohol by volume

The House of Stock has been producing vermouths in Trieste, Italy, since 1884, and its dry vermouth is one of a handful called "white"—that is, completely colorless, just like vodka. Stock uses very dry white wines that are naturally colorless and blends them with Italian brandy and an infusion of herbs, roots, seeds, and spices that are gathered from "all parts of the world" and then steeped for several months.

Tasting Notes

Colorless with faintly herbal nose; light body with palate to follow nose; dry but pleasant fast, full finish.

153

Martini Recipes

———⚜———

WE SEARCHED HIGH AND LOW FOR THE BEST
Martini variation recipes in the country, and
although some of these cocktails won't appeal to staunch
Dry Martini aficionados, we believe that the craft of
mixing drinks is an evolutionary process. The classic
Dry Martini (see below) will never die, but there's always
room for innovative new drinks at our cocktail parties.

The Classic Martini (at left)

AS PREPARED BY DALE DEGROFF
FROM THE RAINBOW PROMENADE BAR,
THE RAINBOW ROOM, NEW YORK

  2 ounces gin
  ¼ ounce dry vermouth
  1 lemon twist, for garnish
  1 olive, for garnish

Stir and strain.

Garnish with lemon twist and olive.

The Absolutely E.T. Martini

FROM THE CRUISE ROOM
IN THE OXFORD HOTEL, DENVER

$1/2$ ounce Absolut vodka

$1/2$ ounce Absolut Citron vodka

$1/2$ ounce Absolut Peppar vodka

$1/2$ ounce Absolut Kurrant vodka

1 lemon twist, for garnish

Stir and strain.

Garnish with lemon twist.

Ajax Tavern's Bloody Mary Martini (at right)

CREATED BY CHRISTOPHER CORRAO,
AJAX TAVERN, ASPEN, COLORADO

Touch of Homemade Rye-Infused
Vermouth (recipe on page 168)

3 ounces Absolut Citron vodka

$1 1/2$ ounces Absolut Peppar vodka

1 lemon citrus olive
or sweet cherry tomato, for garnish

Stir and strain.

Garnish with olive or cherry tomato.

The Alexander Nevsky Martini

CREATED BY CARILLON IMPORTERS, LTD.

2 ounces Stolichnaya Razberi vodka
1 ounce Bombay Sapphire gin
4 fresh raspberries, for garnish

Stir and strain.

Garnish with raspberries.

The Almond Martini

FROM THE MORTON'S
OF CHICAGO MARTINI CLUB

3 ounces Stolichnaya Cristall vodka
Splash of amaretto liqueur
1 almond-stuffed olive, for garnish

Stir and strain.

Garnish with olive.

The Almond Joy Martini

CREATED BY "DIAMOND" DAVE KIERNAN,
JOHNNY LOVE'S, SAN FRANCISCO

Chocolate syrup, for rimming the glass
Sliced almonds, for garnish
1 1/4 ounces Tanqueray Sterling vodka
1/4 ounce Malibu rum
1/4 ounce amaretto liqueur

Pour enough chocolate syrup into a shallow bowl to fill it about ½ inch deep. Invert the rim of a frozen Martini glass in the chocolate syrup so that the interior and exterior of the rim are coated with the syrup. Remove the glass and hold it over the bowl so any extra syrup can drip back into the bowl.

Stick several of the thinly sliced almonds to the inside of the glass. Pour the vodka and rum into a mixing glass half filled with ice cubes.

Stir and strain into the prepared glass. Pour the amaretto down the side of the glass so that it rests in the center of the bottom of the glass.

The Alternating Kurrant Martini

FROM THE PURPLE MARTINI, DENVER

3 ounces Absolut Kurrant vodka
   Splash of Chambord
   Splash of dry vermouth
1 lemon twist, for garnish

Stir and strain.

Garnish with lemon twist.

The Cajun Moon Martini

FROM THE PURPLE MARTINI, DENVER

3 ounces Absolut Peppar vodka
Splash of juice from a jar of
pearl onions
1 pearl onion, for garnish

Stir and strain.

Garnish with pearl onion.

The Cherries Jubilee Martini

FROM THE PURPLE MARTINI, DENVER

3 ounces Ketel One vodka
Splash of amaretto liqueur
1 maraschino cherry, for garnish

Shake and strain.

Garnish with cherry.

The Cherry Kiss Martini

CREATED BY JIM HEWES,
THE ROUND ROBIN BAR AT THE WILLARD
INTERCONTINENTAL HOTEL, WASHINGTON, D.C.

$1/4$ ounce Godiva Chocolate liqueur
1 Martini glass, chilled in the freezer
1 maraschino cherry with its stem
2 ounces Ketel One vodka,
chilled in the freezer

Pour the Godiva liqueur into the frozen Martini glass and swirl it around to coat the glass.

Add cherry to the glass and pour in the vodka.

The Copper Illusion Martini

WINNER OF SEATTLE'S 1994 MARTINI CHALLENGE
CREATED BY MICHAEL R. VEZZONI,
THE FOUR SEASONS HOTEL, SEATTLE

$2^{1}/_{2}$ ounces Beefeater gin

$^{1}/_{4}$ ounce Campari

$^{1}/_{4}$ ounce Cointreau

1 orange twist, for garnish

Stir together for 40 revolutions. Strain into an ice-cold glass.

Garnish with orange twist.

The Dark Cristall Martini

FROM THE CRUISE ROOM
IN THE OXFORD HOTEL, DENVER

3 ounces Stolichnaya Cristall vodka

Splash of Remy Martin

V.S.O.P. cognac

1 lemon twist, for garnish

Stir and strain.

Garnish with lemon twist.

The Down Under Martini

FROM THE PURPLE MARTINI, DENVER

3 ounces gin
  Splash of Pernod
  Dash of Angostura bitters

Stir and strain.

The Fifty-Fifty Martini

FROM THE PURPLE MARTINI, DENVER

1 1/2 ounces gin
1 1/2 ounces dry vermouth
  1 olive or lemon twist, for garnish

Stir and strain.

Garnish with olive or twist.

The Finlandia Blue Moon Martini (at left)

CREATED BY KEVIN CRAFTS FOR
FINLANDIA VODKA'S FASHION MARTINI SERIES

1 1/2 ounces Finlandia vodka
1 1/2 ounces Finlandia Pineapple vodka
  1/2 ounce blue curaçao liqueur
  1 orange twist, for garnish

Stir and strain.

Garnish with orange twist.

The Foley Martini

CREATED BY THE AUTHORS

2 1/2 ounces Stolichnaya Kafya vodka

1/4 ounce sambuca

3 coffee beans, for garnish

Stir and strain.

Garnish with coffee beans.

The French Martini

FROM THE MORTON'S OF CHICAGO
MARTINI CLUB

3 ounces Tanqueray gin

Dash of Pernod

1 lemon twist, for garnish

Stir and strain.

Garnish with lemon twist.

The Gotham Martini (at right)

FROM THE FOUR SEASONS HOTEL, NEW YORK

3 ounces Absolut vodka

1/2 ounce blackberry brandy

1/2 ounce black sambuca

3 blackberries, for garnish

Stir and strain.

Garnish with blackberries.

Homemade Rye-Infused Vermouth

CREATED BY CHRISTOPHER CORRAO,
AJAX TAVERN, ASPEN, COLORADO.

*(This infusion is easy to do. The Bloody Mary Martini
[see p. 150] tastes like a Bloody Mary and looks like a Martini.
Christopher Corrao should be proud of his creation.)*

MAKES 8 OUNCES

1 bottle dry vermouth (750 ml)

8 ounces (1 1/4 cups) rye grains

1/4 cup caraway seeds

2 large pinches of cumin seeds

Pour the vermouth into a 1-liter-size bottle or a large pitcher so there will be room to add the grains. Set aside until needed.

Place a large, dry skillet or sauté pan, preferably nonstick, over medium heat. Add the rye grains, caraway, and cumin seeds. Toast, stirring frequently, until the mixture is very fragrant and a few of the seeds begin to pop, 4 to 5 minutes.

Feed the rye mixture into the vermouth. Cover the bottle and shake to mix well and moisten all of the grains. (If using a pitcher, stir well with a long-handled spoon or a chopstick.) Set aside at room temperature until the vermouth is golden in color and fully flavored from the grain and seed infusion, about 1 day.

Strain the mixture through a sieve into a pitcher. Strain again through a coffee filter or a double thickness of dampened cheesecloth to clarify it further. Store the rye-infused vermouth in the refrigerator.

The Irie Martini

FROM VILLA CHRISTINA, ATLANTA

3 ounces Tanqueray Sterling vodka
   Splash of Tia Maria
   Splash of Grand Marnier
1 coffee bean, for garnish

Stir and strain.

Garnish with coffee bean.

The Italian Martini

FROM THE CRUISE ROOM
IN THE OXFORD HOTEL, DENVER

3 ounces vodka
   Splash of Campari
1 orange slice, for garnish
1 lemon slice, for garnish

Stir and strain.

Garnish with orange and lemon slices.

The Ivory Coast Martini

FROM THE PURPLE MARTINI, DENVER

3 ounces gin
   Splash of white crème de cacao
   Splash of dry vermouth

Stir and strain.

James Bond's Vesper Martini

3 ounces gin
1 ounce Russian vodka
½ ounce Lillet Blanc
1 thin lemon twist, for garnish

Shake and strain.

Garnish with lemon twist.

The Mansion Martini (at right)

FROM THE MANSION ON TURTLE CREEK, DALLAS

Splash of tequila
3 ounces Bombay Sapphire gin or
   Stolichnaya Cristall vodka
2 jalapeño-stuffed olives, for garnish

Rinse the glass with the tequila and discard
the tequila. Stir the liquor over ice until very cold.

Strain into a chilled glass.

Garnish with olives.

The Mardeeni

CREATED WHEN ONE OF THE AUTHORS
WAS VERY THIRSTY

1 tablespoon granulated sugar,
for rimming the glass
1 teaspoon finely grated orange zest,
for rimming the glass
3½ ounces Stolichnaya Oranjh vodka
Splash of Lillet Blanc
1 orange twist, for garnish

Stir the sugar and orange zest together in a wide, shallow bowl. Moisten the outside rim of a well-chilled cocktail glass with a few drops of the vodka. Hold the glass sideways—stem to the left, bowl of the glass to the right—over the bowl.

Sprinkle the sugar and zest mixture onto the moistened rim, turning the stem end as you go to coat the rim evenly all the way around.

Stir the vodka and Lillet over ice; strain into the prepared glass. Garnish with orange twist.

The Markfish Martini

CREATED BY THE AUTHORS

2½ ounces Stolichnaya Kafya vodka

¼ ounce Stolichnaya Zinamon vodka

1 short cinnamon stick, for garnish

Stir and strain.

Garnish with cinnamon stick.

Martini Jo

CREATED BY CHEF JEAN JOHO,
BRASSERIE JO, CHICAGO

3½ ounces Skyy vodka

½ ounce Lillet Rouge

1 orange twist, for garnish

Shake well with ice and strain into a chilled glass.

Rim the glass with orange twist and drop into the drink.

The Melon Martini

FROM THE CRUISE ROOM
IN THE OXFORD HOTEL, DENVER

3 ounces Absolut vodka

1 ounce Midori Melon liqueur

1 orange slice, for garnish

Stir and strain.

Garnish with orange slice.

The Michel Martini (at left)

CREATED BY THE AUTHORS

2 1/2 ounces Stolichnaya Vanil vodka

1/4 ounce Stolichnaya Zinamon vodka

3 redhots (small, red, heart-shaped candies), for garnish

Stir and strain.

Garnish with redhots.

Mikhail's Martini

CREATED BY CARILLON IMPORTERS, LTD.

2 ounces Stolichnaya Kafya vodka

1/4 ounce Stolichnaya Vanil vodka

3 coffee beans, for garnish

Stir and strain.

Garnish with coffee beans.

The Mint Martini

FROM BOULEVARD, SAN FRANCISCO

Colored sugar, for rimming the glass

1 1/2 ounces vodka

Splash of green crème de menthe

1 miniature candy cane, for garnish

Rim the exterior of a chilled Martini glass with colored sugar. Pour the vodka and crème de menthe into a mixing glass filled with ice; stir until chilled. Strain into the prepared glass. Garnish with candy cane.

Norman's Watermelon Martini

CREATED BY NORMAN BUKOFZER,
THE RITZ-CARLTON HOTEL, NEW YORK

2½ ounces gin
¼ ounce Marie Brizard watermelon liqueur
Juice of 1 lime wedge
1 lemon twist, for garnish

Stir and strain.

Garnish with lemon twist.

The Olympic Gold Martini (at right)

WINNER OF SEATTLE'S 1993 MARTINI CHALLENGE

CREATED BY MICHAEL R. VEZZONI,
THE FOUR SEASONS HOTEL, SEATTLE

1 ounce Bombay Sapphire gin
1½ ounces Absolut Citron vodka
⅓ ounce (1 teaspoon) Canton Original
Ginger liqueur
⅙ ounce (½ teaspoon) Martell
Cordon Bleu cognac
1 lemon twist, for garnish

Stir together for 40 revolutions. Strain into
an ice-cold glass.

Garnish with lemon twist.

The Orange Mandarine Martini

FROM THE PURPLE MARTINI, DENVER

3 ounces Stolichnaya Ohranj vodka
Splash of Grand Marnier
1 orange slice, for garnish

Stir and strain.

Garnish with orange slice.

The Pear Martini

FROM THE MORTON'S OF CHICAGO MARTINI CLUB

3 ounces Stolichnaya vodka
$^1/_2$ ounce Poire William eau-de-vie

Stir and strain.

The Ritz Martini

FROM THE RITZ-CARLTON HOTEL, CHICAGO

$2^3/_4$ ounces Stolichnaya vodka or Bombay
Sapphire gin
Splash of dry vermouth
Splash of blue curaçao liqueur

Stir and strain.

The Sake Martini

FROM THE FOUR SEASONS HOTEL, NEW YORK

3 ounces Tanqueray gin

1 ounce sake

1 olive, for garnish

Stir and strain.

Garnish with olive.

The Samara Martini

CREATED BY THE AUTHORS

2¹/₂ ounces Stolichnaya Kafya vodka

¹/₄ ounce Stolichnaya Razberi vodka

1 fresh raspberry, for garnish

Stir and strain.

Garnish with raspberry.

The Scotland Yard Martini

FROM THE CRUISE ROOM
IN THE OXFORD HOTEL, DENVER

3 ounces Beefeater gin

Splash of scotch

1 lemon twist, for garnish

Stir and strain.

Garnish with lemon twist.

La Serre's Tequila Martini (at left)

FROM THE FOUR SEASONS HOTEL, TORONTO

2 ounces Jose Cuervo Gold tequila

$1/2$ ounce Cointreau

$1/2$ ounce Grand Marnier

1 orange twist, for garnish

Stir and strain into a large "fish bowl" snifter.

Garnish with orange twist.

The Silver Fox Martini

FROM THE CRUISE ROOM
IN THE OXFORD HOTEL, DENVER

$1 1/2$ ounces Tanqueray gin

$1 1/2$ ounces Tanqueray Sterling vodka

Splash of dry vermouth

1 olive, for garnish

Stir and strain.

Garnish with olive.

The Skyy Diver Martini

FROM THE CRUISE ROOM
IN THE OXFORD HOTEL, DENVER

3 ounces Skyy vodka

Splash of Rumpleminz Peppermint Schnapps

Stir and strain.

The Staibilizer Martini

FROM VILLA CHRISTINA, ATLANTA

3 ounces Tanqueray Sterling vodka
Splash of Galliano
Splash of Frangelico

Stir and strain.

The Sterling Gold Martini

FROM THE CRUISE ROOM
IN THE OXFORD HOTEL, DENVER

3 ounces Tanqueray Sterling vodka
Splash of Tuaca liqueur
1 orange slice, for garnish

Stir and strain.

Garnish with orange slice.

The Sweet Radish Martini

FROM THE PURPLE MARTINI, DENVER

3 ounces Boodles gin
Splash of Drambuie
1 pearl onion, for garnish

Shake and strain.

Garnish with pearl onion.

182

The Tangerine Martini

FROM THE MORTON'S OF CHICAGO MARTINI CLUB

- 1 orange slice
- 3 ounces Tanqueray Sterling vodka
- $\frac{1}{2}$ ounce Mandarine Napoléon liqueur

Rub the orange slice around the rim of the glass and drop it into the bottom.

Stir and strain.

The Terrace-tini

CREATED BY CHARLES A SHEPHERD,
RIVER TERRACE YACHT CLUB, MEMPHIS

- $\frac{1}{2}$ ounce Grand Marnier
- 4 ounces Bombay Sapphire gin
- 1 orange slice, for garnish

Pour the Grand Marnier into a well-chilled Martini glass and tilt to coat the interior. Stir the gin over ice until very cold; pour into the prepared glass. Thread orange slice onto a sword pick and use as garnish.

The Valencia Martini

FROM PRAVDA, NEW YORK

$4\frac{1}{2}$ ounces gin or vodka
Splash of Dry Sack sherry

Stir and strain.

Bibliography

Amis, Kingsley. *Kingsley Amis on Drink*. New York: Harcourt Brace Jovanovich, Inc., 1973.

Angostura Bitters Complete Mixing Guide. New York: J. W. Wupperman, 1913.

An Anthology of Cocktails together with Selected Observations by a Distinguished Gathering and Diverse Thoughts for Great Occasions. London: Booth's Distilleries, Ltd.

Bayley, Stephen. *Gin*. England: Balding + Mansell, 1994.

Beebe, Lucius. *The Stork Club Bar Book*. New York/Toronto: Rinehart & Company, 1946.

Bishop, George. *The Booze Reader: A Soggy Saga of a Man In His Cups*. Los Angeles: Sherbourne Press, Inc., 1965.

Bullock, Tom. *The Ideal Bartender*. St. Louis: Buxton & Skinner, 1917.

Burke, Harman Burney. *Burke's Complete Cocktail & Drinking Recipes*. New York: Books Inc, 1936.

Carson, Johnny. *Happiness is a dry martini*. New York: Doubleday and Company, Inc., 1965.

The Cocktail Book, A Sideboard Manual for Gentlemen. © L. C. Page & Company, 1900 and 1913. Boston: The Colonial Press, C. H. Simonds Company.

Cotton, Leo, ed. *Old Mr. Boston De Luxe Official Bartender's Guide*. Boston: Mr. Boston Distiller Inc., 1966.

Crockett, Albert Stevens. *The Old Waldorf-Astoria Bar Book*.
New York: A. S. Crockett, 1935.

DeVoto, Bernard. *The Hour*. Cambridge:
Riverside Press, 1948.

Dickens, Cedric. *Drinking with Dickens*.
Goring-on-Thames, England: Elvendon Press, 1980.

Doxat, John. *Stirred-Not Shaken: The Dry Martini*.
London: Hutchinson Benham Ltd., 1976.

Doxat, John. *The Book of Drinking*.
London: Triune Books, 1973.

Duffy, Patrick Garvin. *The Official Mixer's Guide*.
New York: Alta Publications, Inc., 1934.

Elliot, Virginia and Phil D. Stong. *Shake 'Em Up,
A Practical Handbook of Polite Drinking*. Fourth printing,
1932. Brewer and Warren, Inc.

Embury, David A. *The Fine Art of Mixing Drinks*.
2nd edition. New York: Garden City Books, 1952.

Feery, William C. *Wet Drinks for Dry People*. Chicago:
The Bazner Press, 1932.

Gaige, Crosby. *The Standard Cocktail Guide*. New York:
M. Barrows & Company, Inc., 1944.

Grimes, William. *Straight Up or On the Rocks:
A Cultural History of American Drink*. New York:
Simon & Schuster, 1993.

Grossman, Harold J., Revised by Harriet Lembeck.
*Grossman's Guide to Wines, Beers, and Spirits,
sixth revised edition*. New York: Scribner's, 1977.

Hastings, Derek. *Spirits & Liqueurs of the World.*
Constance Gordon Wiener, consulting editor. London:
Footnote Productions, Ltd., 1984.

Johnson, Harry. *New and Improved Bartender's Manual
of How to Mix Drinks.* New York: Harry Johnson, 1888.

Kappeler, George J. *Modern American Drinks: How to Mix
and Serve All Kinds of Cups and Drinks.* New York:
The Merriam Company, 1895.

Kinross, Lord. *The Kindred Spirit, A History of Gin
and the House of Booth.* London:
Newman Neame Limited, 1959.

Lawlor, C. F. *The Mixicologist or How to Mix All Kinds
of Fancy Drinks.* Cleveland: Burrow Brothers, 1897.

Lewis, V. B. *The Complete Buffet Guide or How to Mix Drinks
of All Kinds.* Chicago: M. A. Donahue & Company, 1903.

Lord, Tony. *The World Guide to Spirits, Aperitifs and Cocktails.*
New York: Sovereign Books, 1979.

Mario, Thomas. *Playboy's Host & Bar Book.* Chicago:
Playboy Press, 1971.

Marrison, L. W. *Wines and Spirits.* Baltimore:
Penguin Books, 1957.

Muckensturm, Louis. *Louis' Mixed Drinks with Hints
for the Care and Service of Wines.* New York:
Dodge Publishing Company, 1906.

North, Sterling and Carl Kroch. *So Red The Nose or
Breath in the Afternoon.* New York:
Farrar & Rinehart, 1935.

Pokhlebkin, William. *A History of Vodka.*
Translated by Renfrey Clarke. London/New York:
Verso, 1992.

Rae, Simon, ed. *The Faber Book of Drink, Drinkers and Drinking.* London: Faber and Faber, 1991.

Ray, Cyril, ed. *The Gourmet's Companion.* London:
Eyre & Spottiswood, 1963.

The Reminder. *"Compliments of M. J. Finnegan High Grade Beverages."* Worcester, Massachusetts: 1899.

Straub, Jacques. *Drinks.* Chicago:
Marie L. Straub, 1914.

Thomas, Jerry. *How to Mix Drinks or The Bon Vivant's Companion.* New York: Dick & Fitzgerald, 1862.

Thomas, Jerry. *The Bar-Tender's Guide or How to Mix all Kinds of Plain and Fancy Drinks.* New York:
Fitzgerald Publishing Corporation, 1887.

Townsend, Jack. *The Bartender's Book.* New York:
The Viking Press, 1951.

Vermeire, Robert. *Cocktails How to Mix Them.*
London: Herbert Jenkins Limited.

Magazines

Nation's Restaurant News, 22 April 1996.
National Review, 31 December 1996.

Index